Development Centre Studies

Tackling the Policy Challenges of Migration

REGULATION, INTEGRATION, DEVELOPMENT

OECD

This work is published on the responsibility of the Secretary-General of the OECD. The opinions expressed and arguments employed herein do not necessarily reflect the official views of the Organisation or of the governments of its member countries.

This document and any map included herein are without prejudice to the status of or sovereignty over any territory, to the delimitation of international frontiers and boundaries and to the name of any territory, city or area.

Please cite this publication as:
OECD (2011), *Tackling the Policy Challenges of Migration: Regulation, Integration, Development*
Development Centre Studies, OECD Publishing.
http://dx.doi.org/10.1787/9789264126398-en

ISBN 978-92-64-12631-2 (print)
ISBN 978-92-64-12639-8 (PDF)

Series: Development Centre Studies
ISSN 1563-4302 (print)
ISSN 1990-0295 (online)

Foreword

International migration occupies a prominent place in public debate in both OECD and non-OECD countries. But while many countries of destination increasingly perceive immigration as a threat to social cohesion and try to limit migration inflows, a growing number of countries of origin include emigration in their development strategies, implicitly advocating more labour mobility. The current governance of migration is therefore characterised by a lack of international co-operation, which could be detrimental not only for the countries of emigration, but also for those of transit and destination.

Against this background, and in the context of the OECD Development Centre's programme of work on social cohesion, this book sheds light on three challenges of migration policies today: the regulation of international migration flows; the integration of immigrants, in particular in developing countries; and the impact of labour mobility on development. It is the result of a three-year project entitled "Effective Partnerships for Better Migration Management and Development" funded by the John D. and Catherine T. MacArthur Foundation.

Acknowledgements

Tackling the Policy Challenges of Migration is the product of three years of research of a project entitled "Effective Partnerships for Better Migration Management and Development", benefiting from the generous financial support of the John D. and Catherine T. MacArthur Foundation in Chicago and we are grateful for the opportunity their support provided.

We thank Vanda Legrandgérard for preparing the volume for publication, and Laure Brillaud, Magali Geney, Michèle Girard, Amalia Johnson and Elodie Masson for helping with logistical, administrative and media support. The report also benefited from the devoted and professional work of two trainees, Victoire Lefebvre and Hyeshin Park. We extend our gratitude to Abla Safir, now with the World Bank in Washington DC, for providing useful insights and background work, and to Anne-Lise Prigent of the OECD's Public Affairs and Communication department for extensive comments on the manuscript. Special thanks go to Johannes Jütting and Helmut Reisen for reviewing the manuscript to which Stephen Jessel gave its final form.

We also thank participants in presentations of parts of this work for their suggestions and comments. Previous versions have been presented in OECD workshops in Paris (France), San Jose (Costa Rica), Dakar (Senegal) and Accra (Ghana) as well as in several internal seminars. We would like to thank in particular our colleagues Christian Daude, Jeff Dayton-Johnson, Juan de Laiglesia, Andrew Mold, Papa Amadou Sarr, Henri-Bernard Solignac Lecomte, Jean-Philippe Stijns and Kensuke Tanaka. We also greatly acknowledge the assistance and support we received from our local partners in Accra, the Institute of Statistical, Social and Economic Research (ISSER); in Dakar, the United Nations Development Programme (UNDP); and in San Jose, the Latin American School of Social Sciences (FLACSO).

Sections of the report have been presented in many forms at several external conferences. We are grateful for the comments and feedback from participants at the annual Global Forum for Migration and Development (GFMD) in Athens, Manila and Puerto Vallarta, the World Bank migration workshop in Marseille, the Global Migration Group Symposium in Geneva, the Research Committee on Development Economics (AEL) conference in Hanover, the European Union (EU) roundtable on the Social Aspects of Migration and Development, the Centre de Recherche en Economie Appliquée pour le Développement (CREAD) migration conference in Tipaza, the Association Marocaine d'Études et Recherches sur les Migrations (AMERM) and Institut de Recherche pour le Développement (IRD) migration conference in Rabat, the Paris School of Economics work-in-progress seminar, the Institute of Latin American Studies (ILAS) seminar series at Columbia University, the Ninth Coordination Meeting on International Migration in New York, the EU conference on the management of labour migration in Dakar, the New Opportunities for Research Funding Agency Co-operation in Europe (NORFACE) conference in London and the Centre de Recherche sur les Identités Nationales et l'Interculturalité (CRINI) workshop on migration in Nantes.

Chapter 3 benefited from the time and expertise of many people in Accra. We stand to thank in particular respondents from the many organisations answering our survey on immigrant integration in Ghana: ISSER, the Regional Institute for Population Studies (RIPS) and the Centre for Migration Studies at the University of Ghana, ActionAid, the International Cocoa Initiative, the Centre for the Development of People, the Ghana Immigration Service, the International Organization for Migration (IOM), the United Nations High Commissioner for Refugees (UNHCR), the Cadbury Cocoa Partnership Program, Gesellschaft für Internationale Zusammenarbeit (GIZ) and the National Catholic Secretariat as well as many non-affiliated respondents.

Table of contents

Tables

Figures

Preface

Co-operation over international migration is in gridlock. Despite their growing need for foreign labour OECD countries have implemented increasingly restrictive migration policies, without always taking into account their effects on other countries. But why, exactly, have policy makers been so reluctant to co-operate on migration issues? And what are the implications of non-cooperation? Do migration policies only affect migrant-sending countries or do they also have a cost for the countries implementing them? These questions are occupying increasing political space in OECD countries, and also in many developing countries, which have become, simultaneously, places of origin, transit and destination. Beyond the impact of emigration on development, a number of countries in the South are also facing the challenges of immigration, particularly in terms of social cohesion.

This book addresses how a better comprehensive governance framework can help tackle three complementary policy challenges: the regulation of migration flows, the integration of immigrants, in particular in the South, and the development of migrant-sending countries. It is the culmination of a three-year project entitled "Effective Partnerships for Better Management and Development", primarily financed by the John D. and Catherine T. MacArthur Foundation. The project focused on two main themes: the governance of international migration and the links between emigration and labour markets, and involved two geographical areas: Central America and West Africa.

During this time the authors worked with experts in the field, participated in conferences and organised workshops to pull together a coherent and sound policy framework useful for policy makers, academics, students and the general reader oriented to development policy.

The book begins by providing an overall picture of the current situation of global mobility. Recent international events have helped draw greater attention to how migration is perceived and managed today. The current *modus operandi* is not only harmful for poverty and development; it leads to a lower outcome for everyone – including host countries and migrants. The book then moves towards a policy discussion where the objective is to generate dialogue on the issues at hand to free up the current gridlock.

Mario Pezzini
Director
OECD Development Centre
October 2011

Executive summary

This book provides a contribution to the current debate on international migration by focusing on three elements in the standard migration policy dialogue: the regulation of flows, the integration of immigrants and the impact of labour mobility on development (Figure 0.1).

Figure 0.1. **The policy challenges of international migration**

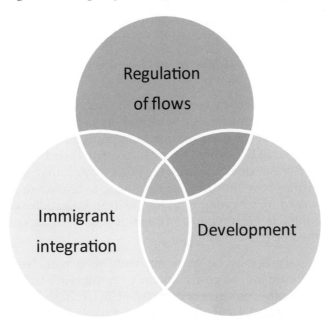

In particular it argues that the current governance of international migration is both insufficient and inefficient. Restrictive and non-cooperative migration policies not only affect development in sending countries but also have counterproductive effects in the countries that implement them. Likewise, the lack of integration policies generates costs for society. The book focuses on South-South migration and highlights the specific risks of neglecting integration in developing countries. It also analyses the effects of emigration on origin-country labour markets and underlines the externalities of immigration policies, that is, their indirect repercussions, in migrant-sending countries.

The regulation challenge

The lack of co-operation between countries of origin, transit and destination raises the challenge of regulating migration flows, especially in the current context of global interdependence. Unlike trade and capital flows, migration policies tend in reality to be unilateral and restrictive:

- While the World Trade Organization (WTO) oversees trade negotiations, and the International Monetary Fund (IMF), along with the Global Financial Board (GFB), manages capital mobility, there is no international organisation regulating migration;

- While free trade applies to trade and capital flows, protectionism dominates migration policy.

The purpose of this book is to analyse the reasons for these differences, by focusing on the asymmetry of benefits between high and low-income countries. It shows that the liberalisation of migration flows benefits workers in countries where skill levels are low, by improving their living conditions in other countries. But this does not work the other way around, as workers from high-wage countries have little interest in moving to low-wage countries. As a result, no organised lobby group is willing to defend the access of workers to foreign labour markets. Negotiations on migration therefore lack an overarching goal, namely the free movement of people.

But this analysis may be more apparent than real. Non-cooperative migration policies are indeed costly, not only for migrants and their countries of origin but also for the countries of destination. In fact, restrictive immigration policies come with financial and human costs. But costly does not mean effective. Strict border controls tend to prevent comings and goings between countries of origin and destination, and translate into high levels of irregular immigration.

The integration challenge

The gradual shift in wealth of the 2000s has contributed to modifying the geography of international migration. Lower transport costs, better and more accessible information and telecommunication technologies, and the growth of incomes in converging economies have helped diminish the financial constraints on emigration, thus enabling potential migrants to move to more distant destinations and in greater numbers. The number of countries affected by international mobility has significantly increased, resulting in a wide diversification of migration corridors.

This book argues that the integration challenge also applies to a growing number of developing countries, which see the benefits of immigration but also the potential cost in terms of social cohesion. It posits that traditional models of integration are not adapted to the South:

- On the one hand, the "assimilation" model lacks relevance, since what is considered as a lack of integration in the North is the normal state of most citizens in the South;

- On the other hand, the "multiculturalism" model does not apply, as problems of social cohesion appear to be more connected to internal fractionalisation than nationality.

But even though integration is not at the centre of concerns, the costs of neglecting it are high. Many developing countries do not consider integration a priority, until problems become insuperable and the political situation ruptures. Côte d'Ivoire is a good illustration of how the escalation of nationalism, in this case through the controversial concept of *ivoirité*, can generate civil unrest and never-ending political crises. The lack of integration policies in the South is often reinforced by discriminatory practices, official and hidden. The high concentration of refugees and migrants stuck in transit in the South contributes to increasing the vulnerability of migrants and the socio-economic costs faced by the "host" society.

The development challenge

Although there can be negative effects on the countries of origin, emigration produces a net benefit not only for the welfare of migrant households, but also for the rest of society.

At the household level, the departure of labour implies a decrease in production. In some cases, namely in rural areas where labour markets are inefficient, this "lost-labour effect" may lead to food insecurity. On the other hand, remittances sent by migrants to the home country help alleviate poverty, and contribute to spurring financial and human capital investment.

At the aggregate level, labour supply may decrease when households receiving money transfers have less incentive to work. But labour outflows also contribute to increasing real wages in the countries of origin. In Honduras, for instance, a 10% rise in emigration helped boost average wages by around 10%.

The book argues that the impact of emigration on labour markets strongly depends on two factors:

- Destination: the benefits are lower when migrants move to another developing country than when they go to richer countries in the North;

- Migration policies in countries of destination: international externalities significantly affect sending-country welfare, not only in the households that send migrants and receive remittances, but also in other households with which they interact.

Tackling the policy challenges of international migration

The policy challenges of migration are closely related. Inefficient regulation can lead to integration problems and reduce the development potential of emigration. Likewise, the contribution of immigrants to the welfare of their countries of origin tends to be inversely proportional to the level of integration in host communities.

But despite these interactions, few countries address all three challenges – regulation, integration, development – together. Furthermore, the current governing system of international migration operates within a non-cooperative framework, which does not take into account the externalities of migration policies on other countries.

The book thus explores the feasibility of implementing a coherent governance framework centred on three complementary objectives: *i)* a more flexible regulation of international migration flows; *ii)* a better integration of immigrants in developing countries; and *iii)* a greater impact of labour mobility on development.

Figure 0.2. **The governance of international migration: objectives**

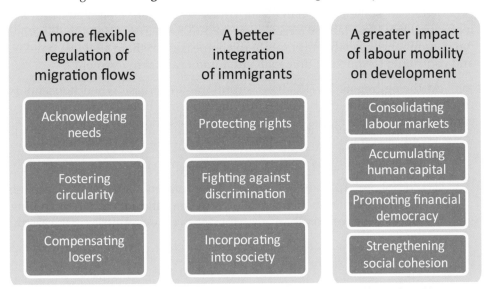

A more flexible regulation of international migration flows

- Because of demographic imbalances, industrialised countries face a growing need for foreign labour, at both the low and high ends of skill levels. A more flexible regulation would therefore benefit the countries of origin as well as those of destination.

- But even the partial withdrawal of migration restrictions would generate costs. Mechanisms are therefore required to compensate those who lose from immigration. A way to lower the adverse impact of immigration is through a system of tax-based compensations, which would finance social safety nets and training programmes.

A better integration of immigrants in developing countries

- South-South migration presents different challenges from South-North, and many countries in the South do not have adequate resources to deal with integration. But despite low financial and administrative capacity, an integration policy can be adapted with current budgetary constraints while maximising the benefits of immigration.

- Facing the challenges of integration entails focusing on three priorities: *i)* the protection of rights; *ii)* the fight against discrimination; *iii)* the incorporation of immigrants into society. The chapter highlights good international practices adopted by developing countries to address them.

A greater impact of labour mobility on development

- Policies to optimise the impact of labour mobility on development in migrant-sending countries should aim to minimise the lost-labour effect and maximise the remittance effect.

- To this end, public authorities should focus on four priorities: *i)* the consolidation of labour markets; *ii)* the accumulation of human capital; *iii)* the promotion of financial democracy; and *iv)* the strengthening of social cohesion.

Effective partnerships for better migration management and development

Finally, the book argues that a comprehensive governance framework should be based on effective partnerships and should rely on four dimensions, which interact to maximise the benefits of international migration:

- **International co-operation.** Unilateral migration policies are both costly and inefficient, while co-operative policies bring benefits to all parties. International co-operation should therefore apply to all levels of governance: bilateral, regional and global.

- **Decentralisation.** Migration policies should also involve local levels through a decentralisation process embedded in local socio-economic development strategies.

- **Inclusiveness.** The governance of migration should include more actors in the decision process, namely non-governmental organisations (NGOs), trade unions, and the private and academic sectors.

- **Policy coherence.** Because inconsistencies between migration policies and other public policies affect their respective efficiency, a coherent governance framework implies that migration policies are co-ordinated with other policies and consider the potential trade-off, for instance between migration and trade policies at the international level and between migration and labour policies at the national level.

Chapter 1

Introduction:
Facts, perceptions, reactions

Abstract

The recent global financial crisis, Arab Spring and famine in Africa have drawn added attention to migration, an issue closely linked to growing global interdependence and environmental factors. Contrary to widespread belief there is more South-South than South-North migration. The financial crisis has made local populations more hostile to immigration, perceived as a threat to jobs and social cohesion. Migration policies have become more restrictive and immigrants greater targets of hostility and prejudice. At the same time, many developing countries seek to benefit from the export of surplus labour and rely heavily on money sent back by migrants. All these factors provide challenges both to sending and recipient countries. Migration strategies are often unilateral and expensive. Three interlocking issues need to be addressed. How can flows be regulated – or is that even possible? Once immigrants have arrived in receiving countries, can they be integrated and if so how? And what is the nexus between migration and development in the immigrants' home countries?

Three recent events have had significant, but opposite, effects on international migration:

1. The **global economic crisis** brought about a decline in labour flows. The impact has been especially hard for the immigrants in countries most affected by the crisis and for their countries of origin.

2. The **Arab Spring** of 2011, which began in Tunisia and rapidly spread to other Middle Eastern and North African (MENA) countries (and even beyond), led to significant movements of population, within and outside the region.

3. The 2011 **famine in the Horn of Africa** has created thousands of refugees, mainly from Somalia, but also from Ethiopia, Kenya and Uganda.

Immigrants have been hit particularly hard by the global economic crisis, since they were the first to lose their jobs in the areas affected by the recession (OECD, 2011). The lack of job opportunities meant that total inflows of immigrants to OECD countries dropped by 13% in 2009 (see Figure 1.1). The decline in immigration was particularly high in Spain (-32%), Ireland (-42%) and the Czech Republic (-49%). By extension, there was a drop in remittances received in most developing countries (-5% on average). Europe and Central Asia (-23%) and Latin America (-12%) were the regions most affected.

Figure 1.1. **Immigration to OECD countries and remittances to developing countries,** 2000-09

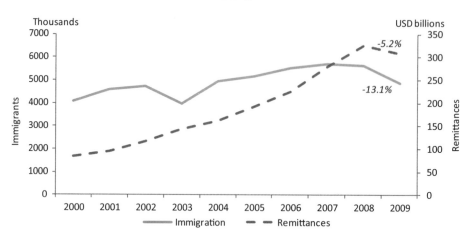

Note: Immigration figures correspond to inflows of foreign population into OECD countries.
Sources: Immigration to OECD countries: OECD (2011); remittances to developing countries: World Bank (2010).

The 2011 Arab Spring raised a dilemma for European governments willing to support democratic transition in the region, but reluctant to welcome fleeing refugees. Images of migrants landing on the Italian island of Lampedusa contributed to the fear of invasion and generated tension within the European Union. But in reality, most flows of people were and remain regional. Tunisia and Egypt, and not Italy and France, have received the highest number of migrants from Libya (see Figure 1.2).

Figure 1.2. **Migrants from Libya, 2011**
Thousands of migrants

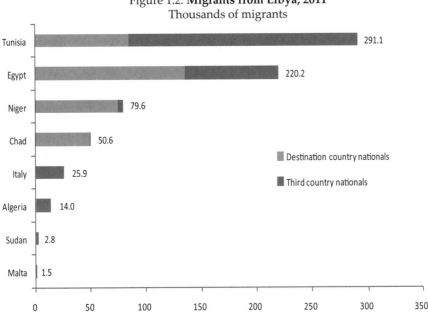

Notes: Number of migrants crossing Libya's borders. Third country nationals include both Libyans and migrants from other countries (mainly from sub-Saharan Africa). Figures are cumulative numbers until 15 September 2011.
Sources: Situation report on Libyan crisis, IOM Middle East North Africa Operations (IOM, 2011).

The 2011 famine in the Horn of Africa affected millions of people who were in need of urgent humanitarian assistance. Because of a severe drought in the region a food crisis threatened the livelihood of more than 13 million people in Ethiopia, Kenya and Somalia (USAID, 2011). By September 2011 the United Nations (UN) had officially declared famine in five regions of southern Somalia and the entire Bay region in Somalia and warned of a spreading risk. As a result thousands of refugees fled to neighbouring countries. Since the beginning of 2011, more than 270 000 Somalis (around 2 000 a day in August) were thus forced to flee to other countries, adding to an already large contingent in Kenya and other countries (see Figure 1.3). According to the UN, around one-third of Somalis were displaced either at the internal or international level (OCHA, 2011).

Figure 1.3. **New Somali arrivals by country of asylum**
Thousands of migrants

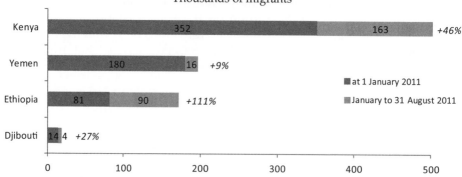

Notes: Figures show increase (%) in Somali refugees in each country during the year (January to 31 August 2011).
Source: UNHCR (2011a).

The global economic crisis, the Arab Spring and the famine in the Horn of Africa have amplified the inherent problems of the current migration system and are thus symptomatic of some of the main facts of contemporary international migration.

The main facts of contemporary migration

One characteristic which overshadows all others is the fact that the world is growing interdependent. It is rare today for a country to be able to manage without engaging in some way with the currents of globalisation, and the multitude of exchanges combined with environmental changes has an impact on migratory patterns. Moreover, immigrants have become extremely vulnerable with little protection and an increasingly hostile locally born workforce. As a consequence, policies have become restrictive, generating more South-South migration. As migration keeps gaining importance, many developing countries have become highly dependent on the benefits of migration for their economies.

Global interdependence increases migration pressures

Political and economic tensions in one part of the planet generate migration pressures in another. In this respect, political transition contributes to increasing the number of internally displaced people (IDPs) and international refugees.

This is because political transition is often accompanied by violence, or because it is suppressed and ends up generating intense backlashes.[1]

Somewhat paradoxically, the transition process to democracy is also a factor of emigration. Elections, for instance, trigger violence in one in four cases.[2] The prospects of freedom abroad are often more tempting than those at home, at least in the initial stages of the transition process. The fall of the Iron Curtain in Eastern Europe was thus followed by a dramatic increase in emigration during the 1990s. In the same way, the Arab Spring produced migratory pressures from various categories of people: from settled immigrants leaving the Arab countries to the locally born fleeing conflict.

Economic interlinkages also constitute an important factor in migration pressures. The process of trade and financial globalisation has undoubtedly given rise to strong economic interdependence between nations. In particular, domestic economic shocks are not constrained by national borders, but rather produce knock-on effects, mainly through trade (Bénassy-Quéré et al., 2009). Although it did not begin in developing countries, the global financial crisis showed how fast interlinkages spread its negative effects through the developing world (Mold et al., 2009).

Adverse economic shocks in developing countries tend to increase international migration flows. Crises in Latin America during the 1990s spurred migration to the US. During the Asian crisis in 1997 and 1998, many workers attempted to find work elsewhere, mostly in the region – even when many of the recipient countries were also affected by the crisis. The continuing crisis in Zimbabwe largely explains the growing exodus to South Africa.

Environmental factors play a growing role in population movements

The volume of displaced people may increase as environmental changes, particularly those induced by global warming, disrupt livelihoods dependent on the stability of local ecosystems. As shown in Figure 1.4, natural disasters have a significant impact on migration flows: not only because livelihoods are destroyed by earthquakes, floods and droughts, but also because natural disasters affect the entire economic activity. The famine in the Horn of Africa is a good illustration of this phenomenon. In 2010, more than 2 million people hit by natural disasters benefited from UN High Commissioner for Refugees (UNHCR) interventions (UNHCR, 2011b).

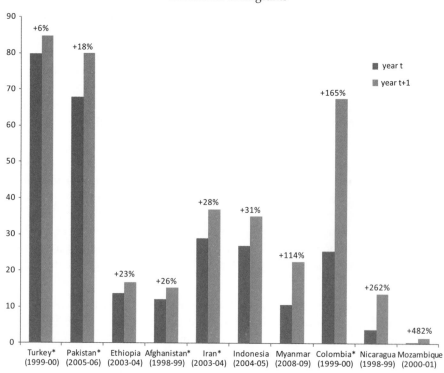

Figure 1.4. **Migration flows after natural disasters**
Thousands of migrants

Notes: Natural disasters in year t: drought in Ethiopia, tsunami in Indonesia, cyclone in Myanmar, storm in Nicaragua, flood in Mozambique, and earthquakes in other countries (*).
Source: Authors' calculations based on the Database on Immigration in OECD countries (DIOC), OECD.

In the long run, estimates on the number of migrants generated by climate change (between 200 million and 1 billion by 2050) are questionable, mainly because they do not consider the capacity of populations to adapt to new conditions, and, above all, gradual environmental changes (UNDP, 2009). The number of migrants will in particular depend on how public policy responds to the environmental challenge. In any case, low-income countries are likely to be more exposed to the consequences of climate change, both because of the higher degree of vulnerability of the poorest populations, and because of the lower responsiveness of public authority.

Although international law does not acknowledge the legal status of "eco-refugees" (Martin, 2010), the community should be prepared to face more internal and international displacements induced by environmental disasters.

The number of South-South migrants is greater than the number of South-North migrants

Contrary to popular belief, most migrants from the South are found in other countries of the South. In 2005 an estimated 58.4 million migrants from developing countries (50.5% of all migrants from the South) lived in another developing country, against 55.9 million (48.2%) in developed economies and 1.5 million (1.3%) in transition economies (see Figure 1.5).[3]

Figure 1.5. **Global stock of international migrants, 2005**
Millions

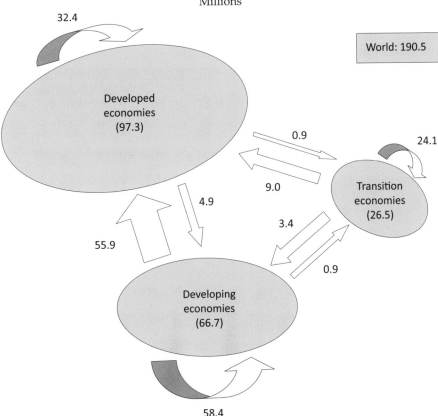

Notes: "Transition economies" include Albania, the countries of the former Soviet Union (minus Estonia, Latvia and Lithuania) and of the former Yugoslavia (minus Slovenia). "Developed economies" encompass all European countries (with the exception of transition economies), plus Australia, Canada, Israel, Japan, New Zealand and the United States (including Puerto Rico and US Virgin Islands). "Developing economies" refers to all other countries.
Source: Own calculations based on Ratha and Shaw (2007), and World Bank (2010). The categorisation between developed, transition and developing countries is based on UNCTAD (2010).

A number of developing countries have thus become net immigration countries, boosting their productive capacity while increasing pressure on social cohesion. Many of the new destination countries represent second-best options as they are closer and exhibit relatively less control over their borders. But many fast-growing economies in the South, such as Argentina, Costa Rica, Ghana, Malaysia, South Africa and Thailand, also represent new magnets for potential migrants, offering better jobs than in their home countries. This was notably the case of Libya, which was at the centre of the European externalisation strategy.[4]

Local populations perceive immigration as a threat to social cohesion

No matter the level of development, new migration flows have produced social tension in countries of transit and destination. By exacerbating anti-immigrant sentiment, the global crisis and the Arab revolts have served as an additional pretext for political exploitation of migration and integration issues. This is particularly striking in several OECD countries, where political debates on multiculturalism and national identity have resurfaced. If xenophobia is indicative of low levels of social cohesion (Ruedin and D'Amato, 2011), many countries still have some way to go before they reach acceptable levels.

Figure 1.6. **Attitudes towards immigration in the UK, 2009-10**

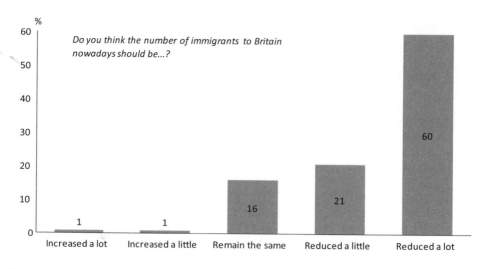

Source: www.migrationobservatory.ox.ac.uk, based on the Citizenship Survey, 2009-10.

Figure 1.6 displays answers to the question *"Do you think the number of immigrants to Britain nowadays should be .... ?"*, from the British Citizenship Survey in 2009-10. According to 81% of respondents born in the UK, this number should be reduced. This response to the crisis is representative of many OECD countries. In light of fears for the security of their jobs as well as their safety, anti-immigrant sentiment rose among the locally born in almost every OECD country, including historically tolerant societies such as Norway. Citing a study conducted by TNS Gallup, *Aftenposten*, a major newspaper in Norway, claimed that the number of Norwegians who want a stop to immigration has never been so high.[5] The rise has triggered a domino effect with many countries declaring that their integration policies over the last 20 to 30 years have all but failed.

In developing countries too, anti-immigrant riots and mass deportations have been on the rise. In 2008, violent attacks against immigrants were reported in several parts of South Africa. Similarly in Gabon and Malaysia, for instance, locals have been vocal and physical in their intolerance of the idea of importing foreign labour. Deportations of immigrants back and forth between Angola and the Democratic Republic of Congo (DRC) have continued. In 2011, dozens of Bangladeshi immigrants in the United Arab Emirates (UAE) were deported from the country for striking for better wages. Conflict between immigrants and the locally born is at the core of the crisis in Côte d'Ivoire. Anti-immigrant attitudes help establish the basis for violations of immigrants' rights by authorities in Mexico and Morocco, for instance, eager to win popularity from voters. In many Gulf Cooperation Council (GCC) countries and in Malaysia, locals are growing intolerant about the preference employers give to hiring immigrants.

Migration policies tend to be increasingly restrictive

Policies limiting immigration flourished during and after the crisis, and were reinforced by the Arab Spring. Even the right to the free movement of people within the Schengen area in Europe has been questioned. In 2011, for instance, Denmark suspended the agreement and re-introduced border controls while France also considered the idea.

In the South, policies are also becoming more protective of the local population. Since 2008, the Malaysian government has officially aimed at reducing the employment of migrants. Fences are being built in different parts of the world, from Costa Rica to India, to keep "intruders" from entering the country. Identification card systems are being implemented to distinguish those who belong from those who do not.

In the event, many of these policies sometimes come at a cost for local employers. In Thailand, the crackdown on irregular migration from neighbouring countries has left many agricultural employers searching for much-needed labour. The government has had to bend the rules to allow non-regularised migrants to continue working and give them more time to apply for regularisation. A similar situation is developing in the GCC countries, where the lack of available labour arising from stricter policies has led to a decrease in productivity and more bargaining power for emigrant countries. These tensions are emblematic of the lack of international co-operation on migration issues.

Many immigrants suffer high levels of vulnerability

In most countries affected by the economic crisis, unemployment increased faster for foreign than for native-born workers (OECD, 2011). As the economy cooled down, many firms were forced to shed labour. Immigrants were the first to go as it was easier to revoke their contracts, both legally and politically. The fact that a number of undocumented immigrants were working informally, made it easier for employers to annul any pre-existing agreement.

The conflict in Libya also exposed the fact that many immigrants, particularly those stuck in transit, are vulnerable to violations of human rights. Many were forced to return home or move to neighbouring countries. A bilateral agreement signed between Italy and Libya, for instance, allowing Italy to repatriate irregular immigrants to Libya, increased the danger.[6] As the detention centres in Libya are poorly maintained, they only help exacerbate the situation as authorities sell the detainees to traffickers, who then help migrants attempt to cross to Italy again, restarting the vicious cycle. The price migrants pay to traffickers is often exorbitant, sometimes amounting to several times any eventual monthly wage. Following the conflict, many immigrants were forced to stay or emigrate illegally, as their passports were kept by their employers.

With little in terms of representation, immigrants find themselves in situations where their rights are not defended. This happens in both OECD and non-OECD countries. In the Dominican Republic, children born to the darker-skinned Haitians are denied citizenship on the basis that their parents were in "transit" when they were born (Human Rights Watch, 2002). In Mexico immigrants are often forced into economic circumstances involving illicit goods and gang violence. In Saudi Arabia, immigrants from Asia are subjected to death penalties, without recourse even to the consular services of their countries. Many of the crimes allegedly follow defensive attacks in response to attempted rape and torture by the immigrants' employers. As many as 60% of Indonesians who go overseas to work face serious problems, ranging from physical abuse to not being paid, being killed on the job or committing suicide out of despair.[7] Indeed, in 2009 the Indonesian government banned the deployment of domestic helpers to Malaysia, in response to cases of abuse. Many employers also fail to pay their workers. In a survey of 169 migrant workers in Qatar, one-third reported regularly not getting paid on time and 35% reported they were working seven days a week.[8]

A number of developing countries have become dependent on emigration and remittances

In some cases, developing countries see migration as a potential source of development finance, through private remittances, and have consequently geared part of their economies into maximising the return. This approach has been a trend in Asia, notably in the Philippines, but increasingly in Bangladesh, Nepal, Sri Lanka and Viet Nam as well. The Colombo Process has formalised co-ordination and information-sharing between these countries. In Latin America too, countries have become dependent on this model. In Honduras, Guyana, El Salvador and Haiti, remittances represent more than 15% of GDP. While most Latin American countries are highly dependent on the United States the migrant stock is gradually diversifying to include countries such as Spain, France and Canada.

At the other end, many countries struggling with reform have used migration as a safety valve to reduce internal pressure: emigration in the case of the labour market and remittances to fuel the economy. The 2009 drop in remittances, coupled with the enforcement of immigration restrictions in OECD countries, affected developing countries relying on this strategy. As policies become stricter, it will be increasingly harder to rely on a *laissez-faire* approach for a migration-for-development strategy, particularly as industrialised countries gradually turn to a points-system of immigration aimed at luring high-skilled migration and keeping lower-skilled migrants out.

The policy challenges of international migration

The current governance of international migration leads to a sub-optimal equilibrium, not only affecting migrants themselves as well as their countries of origin, but also countries of destination.

As underlined above, the growing trend of restricting movements of population contributes to making international migrants more vulnerable.

- Migration routes have become more dangerous, encouraging migrant smuggling and human trafficking;

- Stricter border controls increase the number of undocumented immigrants, making the protection of migrant rights more difficult;

- Even migrants with official documentation may find it more difficult to integrate in a context of rejection and intolerance.

Non-cooperative migration policies also impact on migrant-sending countries, since labour mobility can no longer act as a safety valve for the labour market. Moreover, remittance flows to developing countries are affected by labour restrictions, thus reducing welfare in origin countries, particularly at the household level.

But migrant-receiving countries also pay the cost of stringent border controls. Not only because restrictions imply financial and administrative costs, but also because they do not succeed in deterring immigrants from developing countries from bypassing controls and penetrating irregularly into the territory. This strategy gives rise to a vicious circle, where more protection against immigration translates into increasing numbers of undocumented immigrants. As a result, countries of destination face more migration-related problems and the rejection of immigrants by locals is higher.

Unilateral migration policies also have as a consequence that origin countries are reluctant to co-operate on migration issues, namely the control of outflows, thus amplifying the efficiency costs of such policies. This is why migration strategies need to be revised, taking into account three policy challenges that plague the current governance of migration: the regulation of flows, the integration of immigrants and the links with development.

The next three chapters develop a specific aspect of each of these challenges:

- **Chapter 2** focuses on the global governance of migration. It argues that, unlike trade and capital flows, migration is characterised by the lack of a regulating body and by protectionist policies. This can be explained by the asymmetry in the benefits derived by high and low-wage countries. But the lack of international co-operation has a cost, not only for migrant-sending countries but also for those implementing restrictions.

- **Chapter 3** concentrates on immigrant integration in the South. It shows that integration issues need to be analysed from a different angle than is the case in South-North contexts. Although most migrants from the South are found in the South, immigrant integration is not a current priority for many policy makers in developing countries. However, neglecting integration may be more costly than in the North when tensions spiral out of control.

- **Chapter 4** looks at the link between migration and development, with specific interest paid to the labour market. It argues that the trade-off in the household between labour resources lost to emigration and increasing income from remittances implies changes in labour supply for the household members staying behind. In the aggregate, the positive impact of emigration on wages in the home country is an important dimension of development and economic convergence between poorer and richer countries.

Chapter 5 then provides an overview of policies deriving directly from the analysis of these chapters. It advocates a redefinition of the objectives of migrations policies, which should be oriented towards: *i)* a more flexible regulation of international migration flows; *ii)* a better integration of immigrants in the South; and *iii)* a greater impact of labour mobility on development.

Finally, **Chapter 6** argues that the governance of international migration should rely on effective partnerships and include four dimensions: *i)* international co-operation; *ii)* decentralisation; *iii)* inclusiveness; and *iv)* policy coherence.

Notes

1. According to the US Institute of Peace, around 50% of all peace agreements unravel after five years, thus giving rise to increase periods of violence. In www.usip.org/programs/initiatives/managing-political-transitions-africa.

2. The US Institute of Peace argues that *"electoral violence tends to persist as underlying causes remain unresolved."* In addition, *"persistent electoral violence arguably reduces the consolidation of democratic norms and the prospects for long-term for durable peace and stability."* (ibid.)

3. The data used for this analysis originate from a joint venture between the University of Sussex and the World Bank to build a bilateral migration matrix with estimates of the stock of migrants by country of origin and destination (see Ratha and Shaw, 2007, for more details). Based on census data, these estimates are subject to the inherent limits of counting migrants (Dumont and Lemaitre, 2005; Dumont *et al.*, 2010). The number of undocumented migrants and the differences from one country to another in the definition itself of "immigrant" make the exercise more difficult. Estimating South-South flows is even more complicated than in the case of developed countries as borders are generally more porous than in the North, and statistical systems subject to more deficiencies.

4. In exchange for their co-operation on migration issues, origin and transit countries benefit from increased development assistance, independently of poverty reduction objectives (AidWatch, 2010).

5. On 22 July 2011 a Norwegian citizen carried out a mass slaughter of scores of his compatriots with the aim of forcing the government to abandon its multicultural model.

6. Migrants' Rights Network, 16 May 2011, "EU policy: bilateral agreements with Libya have increased the danger to migrants during the current upheaval".

7. *The Economist*, 3 July 2011, "Beheading the Golden Goose". The figure of 60% was reported by Migrant Care, an Indonesian NGO.

8. *Gulf Times*, 6 March 2011, "One-third of Asian workers not paid on time: survey".

References

AidWatch (2010), *Penalty against Poverty: More and better EU Aid Can Score Millennium Development Goals*, Concord AidWatch Initiative.

Bénassy-Quéré, A., Y. Decreux, L. Fontagné and D. Khoudour-Castéras (2009), "Economic Crisis and Global Supply Chains", *CEPII working paper*, No. 2009-15, CEPII, Paris.

Dumont, J.C. and G. Lemaître (2005), "Counting Immigrants and Expatriates in OECD Countries: A New Perspective", *OECD Social, Employment and Migration Working Papers*, No. 25, OECD, Paris.

Dumont, J.C., G. Spielvogel and S. Widmaier (2010), "International Migrants in Developed, Emerging and Developing Countries: An Extended Profile", *OECD Social, Employment and Migration Working Papers*, No. 113.

Human Rights Watch (2002), "Illegal People": Haitians and Dominico-Haitians in the Dominican Republic, Human Rights Watch, New York, NY.

IOM (International Organization for Migration) (2011), "Response to the Libyan Crisis, External Situation Report", 15 September 2011, IOM.

Martin, S. (2010), "Climate Change, Migration and Governance", *Global governance: A Review of Multilateralism and International Organizations*, VoL. 16, No. 3, pp. 397-413.

Mold, A., S. Paulo and A. Prizzon (2009), "Taking Stock of the Credit Crunch: Implications for development finance and global governance", *Working Paper* No. 277, OECD Development Centre, Paris.

OCHA (Office for the Coordination of Humanitarian Affairs) (2011), "Somalia – Famine and Drought", *Situation Report*, No. 14, OCHA, New York, NY.

OECD (2011), *International Migration Outlook 2011*, OECD, Paris.

Ratha, D. and W. Shaw (2007), "South-South Migration and Remittances", *World Bank Working Paper*, No. 102, World Bank, Washington, DC.

Ruedin, D. and G. D'Amato (2011), "Social Cohesion Challenges in Europe", *Research report background paper for EU-US Immigration Systems 2011/04*, Migration Policy Institute, Washington, DC.

THE MIGRATION OBSERVATORY (2011), "Citizenship Survey 2009-2010", www.migrationobservatory.ox.ac.uk.

UNCTAD (United Nations Conference on Trade and Devleopment) (2010), *UNCTAD Handbook of Statistics*, United Nations, New York, NY, and Geneva .

UNDP (United Nations Development Programme) (2009), *Human Development Report 2009. Overcoming Barriers: Human Mobility and Development*, UNDP, Palgrave Macmillan, New York, NY.

UNHCR (United Nations High Commissioner for Refugees) (2011a), "East & Horn of Africa Update, Somali Displacement Crisis at a glance", 13 September 2011, UNHCR, Geneva.

UNHCR (2011b), "UNHCR Global Trends 2010", UNHCR, Geneva.

USAID (United States Agency for International Development) (2011), "Horn of Africa – Drought", Fact Sheet No. 12, USAID, Washington, DC.

WORLD BANK (2010), *Migration and Remittances Factbook 2011*, World Bank, Washington, DC.

Chapter 2

Global governance and the regulation of migration flows

Abstract

At a time when national policies on immigration are becoming increasingly restrictive no comprehensive international legal framework governing migration exists. Unlike trade and capital flows, which are subject to governance and regulation, immigration is not. Though there has been growing interest in the link between immigration and development, receiving countries often seek to use development aid to reduce immigration. A major problem is that immigration is asymmetrical: workers from the North are not interested in going to countries of the poorer South. Furthermore public opinion in the North, especially among the poorest and least educated, is increasingly hostile to immigration even if government policies, perhaps driven by organised lobbies, do not fully reflect public attitudes. Non-cooperative policies may even be counter-productive. Restrictive policies are often expensive, have human costs and do not necessarily work. Economists point to the benefits of immigration, though their views are not often heard.

Are the formulation and implementation of migration policies enough to make it possible to talk about a governance of international migration? Strictly speaking, they are. Public governance is defined as "the exercise of political, economic and administrative authority" (OECD, 2009a). The exercise of such authority within the framework of migration regulation can thus be termed "governance". But by their very nature, migration policies have repercussions on other countries. For instance, when a government unilaterally closes its borders to foreign workers, emigration can no longer act as a safety valve for the problems of other nations. The governance of migration therefore requires a minimum level of co-ordination between receiving and sending countries, at least in theory.

In practice, "there is no comprehensive international legal framework governing the cross-border movement of people" (OECD, 2004). Most migration policies are taken unilaterally with the externalities generated by such policies on other countries not considered at the time their objectives are defined. By way of comparison, it is as if a country were to adopt trade restrictions without analysing their impact on its main partners or the risk in terms of economic growth.

But while the World Trade Organization (WTO) and the G20 offer persistent reminders of the risk of trade barriers on international stability, few are the voices warning about the counterproductive effects of migration restrictions. So why do sending and receiving countries not sit down together to discuss migration issues, in the same way they do it for trade and finance?

It is true that immigration has become a very sensitive issue, increasingly associated – rightly or wrongly – with problems of unemployment, public security and integration. But are migration-related problems the cause of the lack of international co-operation, or is it the other way around? In other words, could the lack of co-operation be the origin of the problems?

This chapter argues that unlike trade and capital flows, regulated by international organisations and the *laissez-faire* principle, the governance of migration is characterised by the lack of a regulating body and by protectionist policies. The main reason why the two regimes are so different is linked to the asymmetry in the benefits derived by high and low-wage countries. However, the lack of international co-operation has a cost, not only for migrant-sending countries but also for the countries of destination implementing restrictions.

A non-cooperative governance framework

The global governance of migration consists of two main dimensions: the regulation of flows and the link between migration and development.[1] These two dimensions are, in essence, complementary. Indeed, the impact of labour mobility on development, as highlighted in Chapter 4, strongly depends on migration policies in the countries of destination.

The international regulation of migration flows

There are two significant differences between the governance of international migration and the governance of trade and capital flows. The first concerns the existence or not of a regulating body; the second is related to tendencies in international political principles: free trade or protectionism.

While the WTO oversees trade negotiations and helps settle disputes, there is no international organisation regulating migration. There is also no institution able to address international migration issues in the same way that the International Monetary Fund (IMF) or the newly-created Global Financial Board (GFB) do for capital flows. Despite improvements over the last decade in migration management, the International Organization for Migration (IOM) has been mainly designed to provide migration services to member states and migrants, such as recruitment, selection and orientation, but not with the goal of co-ordinating and supervising migration policies.

Other international organisations are also concerned with migration issues, such as the International Labour Organization (ILO), charged with the design and supervision of international labour standards, and the United Nations High Commissioner for Refugees (UNHCR), mandated to lead and co-ordinate the protection of international refugees. But their role is relatively limited with respect to the regulation of migration flows. For instance, the *1998 ILO Declaration on Fundamental Principles and Rights at Work,* which defines a set of core labour standards considered basic human rights, does not include standards on migrant labour.

In this respect, the two ILO Conventions that explicitly cover migrant workers, that is, the *1949 Migration for Employment Convention* (No. 97) and the *1975 Migrant Workers Convention* (No. 143), have only been ratified by 49 and 23 countries, respectively (as of October 2011).[2] And the *1990 UN International Convention on the Protection of All Migrant Workers and Members of their Families* has, so far, 45 ratifications, none of them by Northern industrialised countries.[3]

While the globalisation of trade and finance rests on the *laissez-faire* principle, migration policies are increasingly restrictive. Since the end of World War-II and in the framework of the General Agreement on Tariffs and Trade (GATT), international negotiations led to the gradual dismantling of tariff and non-tariff barriers. Likewise, the financial globalisation process has been accompanied, under the auspices of the IMF, by the removal of foreign exchange controls and international barriers to capital mobility. By contrast, the international regulation of migration flows over the last four decades has led to the rise of barriers to labour mobility, at least at the global level (see Box 2.1).

Box 2.1. Trade and capital vs. migration at the regional level

While at the global level most countries impose restrictions on population movements, at the regional level the principle of free circulation prevails. Table 2.1 shows that in Africa, Europe and Latin America, people are free to circulate, at least in theory. In Asia free trade agreements are still being negotiated and most governments opt for bilateral rather than regional agreements in respect of labour mobility. One notable case of a regional free trade area with capital mobility, but without complete labour mobility, is the North American Free Trade Agreement (NAFTA). This can be explained by the asymmetry in benefits described below (see in particular Figure 2.1).

But the existence of regional agreements on labour mobility does not always mean that free circulation really applies. In practice, there are many restrictions to regional free circulation.

As an example, discussion in West Africa on the creation of an integrated region through migration is an old story. But lack of political will and a variety of national priorities have never made it possible. Although ECOWAS endorsed the free movement of labour in 1979, initial individual country reaction was to restrict mobility at its own borders, and the protocol of free movement of persons was never fully and truly implemented. In fact, several countries (Senegal, 1990, Benin, 1998, and Côte d'Ivoire, 1999) have called up obscure clauses in the protocol in the past, in effect cancelling the rights that accompany it (OECD, 2008).

Even in Europe, where the process is at an advanced level, regional mobility remains relatively low compared, for instance, to the United States. Differences in languages and cultures matter, but probably do not explain all of the difference. Furthermore, recent discussions on intra-regional mobility within the Schengen area, as a consequence of the 2011 Arab Spring and the fear of invasion (see Chapter 1), show that free circulation is never irrevocably established.

Table 2.1. **Trade, capital and labour mobility in regional agreements**

	Regional Agreements	Type	Capital mobility	Labour mobility
Africa	Common Market for Eastern and Southern Africa (COMESA)	FTA	Yes	Yes
	East African Community (EAC)	CU	Yes	Yes
	Economic Community of West African States (ECOWAS)	FTA	Yes	Yes
	Southern African Development Community (SADC)	FTA	No	No
Asia	ASEAN Free Trade Area (AFTA)[a]	FTA	Yes	No
	South Asian Free Trade Agreement (SAFTA)	FTA	No	No
Europe	European Free Trade Association (EFTA)	EIA	Yes	Yes
	European Economic Area (EEA)	EIA	Yes	Yes
	European Union (EU)	EIA	Yes	Yes
Latin America	Andean Community (CAN)	CU	Yes	Yes
	Caribbean Community and Common Market (CARICOM)	EIA	Yes	Yes
	Central American Common Market (CACM)	CU	Yes	Yes (CA-4)[b]
	Southern Common Market (MERCOSUR)	EIA	No	Yes
North America	North American Free Trade Agreement (NAFTA)	FTA	Yes	No[c]
Others	Gulf Cooperation Council (GCC)	CU	No	Yes
	Commonwealth of Independent States (CIS)	FTA	No	No
	Pan-Arab Free Trade Area (PAFTA)	FTA	No	No

Notes: FTA = Free Trade Agreements; CU = Customs Union; EIA = Economic Integration Agreement.
a) At the 12th Association of Southeast Asian Nations (ASEAN) Summit in January 2007, the leaders agreed to hasten the establishment of the ASEAN Economic Community by 2015 and to transform ASEAN into a region with free movement of goods, services, investment, capital and skilled labour.
b) CA-4 = Central American Four (El Salvador, Guatemala, Honduras and Nicaragua).
c) Temporary entry for certain classes of professional workers and business people.

The 1973 oil crisis marked the end of the relatively open international migration regime that characterised the post-war period of reconstruction: with the crisis, most industrialised countries closed their doors to new foreign workers and opted for a strategy based on temporary labour and financial incentives for migrants to return to their home countries.

Even though other forms of migration flourished, namely under asylum and family reunification programmes, this strategy has not varied much over the last decades (Hatton and Williamson, 2005). On the contrary, barriers to immigration – aimed particularly at developing countries – have tended to increase, not only at the administrative level (for instance with the external borders of the Schengen area), but also physically with the erection of walls, such as those at the US-Mexican or Spanish-Moroccan borders.

The international reaction to the global economic crisis exemplifies the difference in treatment between trade and financial issues on the one hand and migration issues on the other. From the very beginning of the crisis, the WTO and academic economists have expressed concern about the risk of a resurgence of trade protectionism (Baldwin and Evenett, 2009). Moreover, the leaders of the G20 committed not to repeat the mistakes of the Great Depression, when "beggar-thy-neighbour" policies hastened the collapse of world trade and, by extension, global output.

At the financial level, while international reaction to the crisis led the G20 to strengthen regulation and prudential control, and to promote co-operation by creating the Global Financial Board, there was no talk of limiting capital mobility. By contrast, the global economic crisis gave rise to anti-immigration measures, under the pressure – real or supposed – of public opinion (Khoudour-Castéras, 2009).

Fighting against undocumented immigrants has thus become one of the top priorities on the migration-policy agenda since the beginning of the crisis. Recent legislation in Italy (2009)[4] and in the US state of Arizona (2010)[5] has made irregular immigration a crime punishable by fines and imprisonment, and deportations from Europe to Africa or from the United States to Latin America have increased (Chamie and Mirkin, 2010; Flores Sánchez and Martín Rivero, 2009).

Countries of immigration hit by the crisis tried to reduce regular immigration too. In 2009, for instance, the United States Senate adopted the Employ American Act, which limited the possibility for companies receiving public subsidies, in particular financial institutions, of hiring high-skilled foreign workers, even on a temporary basis (Friedman, 2009). Migration policies have also materialised into voluntary return programmes. Countries such as the Czech Republic, Japan and Spain offer financial incentives to immigrants who accept to return, for a long-term period, to their country of origin (OECD, 2010).

Beyond the debate on their legitimacy, it is likely that such measures suffer from a ratchet effect, arising from the difficulty that policy makers face in removing restrictive legislation on immigration. As a result, whereas the recent crisis has been the opportunity to reaffirm free trade principles and to strengthen international financial co-operation, the regulation of migration flows has become increasingly unilateral and the possibilities of co-operation more remote. Most notably it has potentially jeopardised the link between migration and development.

The link between migration and development

While the regulation of migration flows has been characterised by a lack of international co-operation, there has been a growing interest over the last decade in migration and development issues. Such interest materialised in 2006 with the United Nations High-Level Dialogue on Migration and Development, a state-led process aimed at building effective partnerships to leverage the impact of international migration on development.[6] Even though the High-Level Dialogue did not translate into formal co-operation mechanisms (Martin *et al.*, 2007), it contributed to furthering global discussions on migration issues and gave rise to the Global Forum on Migration and Development (see Box 2.2).

Box 2.2. **The Global Forum on Migration and Development**

The Global Forum on Migration and Development (GFMD) is not meant to produce agreements or normative decisions, but rather to gather representatives from the countries of origin, transit and destination to discuss best policy practices. The annual event has been held in Brussels (2007), Manila (2008), Athens (2009), Puerto Vallarta (2010) and Geneva (2011).

So far the process has resulted in a series of policy recommendations oriented towards the improvement of migrant conditions, better inclusion of migrants – in particular through diasporas – into development strategies, and a better coherence of migration and development policies. But despite the efforts, there is still a long way to go before a global consensus on migration and development is reached.

- The **non-binding nature of the Forum** is a point of disagreement between those who consider the flexibility of the process as a chance to move forward on such a sensitive issue as migration, and those who see it as an obstacle to concrete action towards a more co-operative governance framework.

- The **role of civil society** needs to be clarified, as the delegates of civil society complain that their recommendations are not taken into account by governments. The fact that delegates from both sides barely meet is indicative of the many misunderstandings between them, particularly on the role of migrants, as well as their status and position in society.

- The **protection of the rights of migrants** is a controversial issue. Most countries of immigration consider that migrants who try to cross borders irregularly violate immigration laws, and therefore cannot blame states for the difficulties they face by doing so. By contrast, countries of origin, as well as most representatives from civil society, reckon that by implementing increasingly restrictive migration policies, countries of destination are responsible – even indirectly – for the violations of human rights that affect migrants.

- In theory, sending and receiving countries share the same interests concerning migration and development issues. In this respect the GFMD enables all parties to co-ordinate their policies to maximise the benefits of mobility. In practice, there is a discrepancy on the **direction of the link between migration and development.** While a number of industrialised countries see development as a way to contain immigration, many developing countries consider emigration as an instrument for development.

- The Global Forum, as its name indicates, focuses on the link between migration and development, but there is a **lack of discussion on the regulation of migration flows**. Nevertheless, migration policies are implicitly at the centre of discussions. It is difficult to leverage migration for development if people are not allowed to move.

In parallel with the GFMD, the Global Migration Group (GMG), an inter-institutional group of agencies involved in migration-related activities, was established in 2006, with the purpose of providing analysis to its members, promoting the application of global and regional instruments and norms, and encouraging the co-ordination of migration and development policies. It has also served as a focal point for many of its members' recent initiatives, as advocated by the 2007 Report of the UN Secretary-General *International*

Migration and Development, which in particular concludes that relevant bodies, agencies, funds and programmes of the United Nations system should carry out migration-related activities such as "building capacity, assisting in the formulation and implementation of migration policies, and promoting practices that maximise the positive impact of migration on development and minimise its negative outcomes" (UN Secretary-General, 2007: 19). In the same perspective, the 2009 Human Development Report *Overcoming Barriers: Human Mobility and Development* proposes policies to enhance the human development impact of migration (UNDP, 2009).

The renewed interest in the migration-development nexus has come with an impressive amount of – sometimes conflicting – literature on the role of emigration as a driving force for (or a hindrance to) economic and social development. It has also resulted in the inclusion of migration and development issues in the international co-operation framework of several OECD countries.

In France, for instance, one of the stated missions of the Ministry of the Interior[7] consists of supporting economic and social initiatives that enable migrants to take part in the development of their home countries. Similarly, the Dutch Ministry of Foreign Affairs has a specific division in charge of international migration and development, and the Spanish Agency for International Co-operation and Development (AECID) has included migration among its key intervention channels. Even more significantly, the 2008 European Council, in Brussels, adopted the European Pact on Immigration and Asylum, which emphasises the importance of involving immigrants in development projects, and co-ordinating migration and development policies to benefit migrant-sending areas.

The formulation of policies linking migration and development is based on the idea that it is possible to enhance welfare in migrant-sending countries through the efficient management of international movements, but also – at least implicitly – that development should contribute, in the shorter or longer term, to reducing migration pressures from developing countries. Such assumption manifests itself in the so-called co-development policies (Khoudour-Castéras, 2010).

The notion of co-development first appeared in the 1980s, mainly under the influence of French diplomacy. The purpose was to give a new direction to international co-operation programmes, and to move from the logic of official development assistance, according to which Northern countries set the measures they deem necessary for the development of the South, to the logic of shared management of resources and responsibilities (Malgesini, 2001).

In the context of global interdependence, co-development implies that economic, social and environmental problems in the South may turn into a burden for other countries, while the improvement in living conditions in developing countries has positive repercussions on the international community. Therefore, industrialised countries have a direct interest in the development of the poorest nations in the world, such interest being particularly manifest with regard to migration.[8] Co-development is actually based on the idea that public authorities should spur the financial and human capital gains associated with migration by mobilising migrants to contribute to the socio-economic development of both their host and origin countries (Naïr, 1997).

But while the notion of co-development emphasises the positive role of migration in the development of both receiving and sending countries, it has increasingly become an anti-immigration strategy. The insistence of European authorities on financing productive – meaning job-creating – projects instead of investing in social or educative ones, is thus symptomatic of the use of co-development as a containment policy (Daum, 1998). Likewise, return policies reflect developed countries' temptation not to integrate new immigrant populations into society (Weil, 2002).

At the same time, there has been a growing tendency to trade development aid for migration controls, in particular through the externalisation of migration policies. In exchange for their co-operation on migration issues, origin and transit countries benefit from increased development assistance, independently of poverty reduction objectives (AidWatch, 2010). This is notably the case of Cape Verde, which, because of its strategic position off the west coast of Africa, has benefited from increasing development assistance from European countries, first among them Spain, to make Frontex (European Union border security agency) operations possible in its territorial waters.

More generally, many North-South co-operation policies rest on the illusion that economic development constitutes the best way to reduce immigration. In such a perspective, an increase in official development assistance (ODA) or in trade preferences is supposed to work in favour of both development and of migration reduction (Böhning, 1994). However, experience shows that development aid and trade liberalisation policies tend to increase emigration in developing countries, since the improvement in living conditions that usually follows such policies contributes to relieving the financial constraint associated with the decision to migrate (Berthélemy et al., 2009; de Haas, 2007; OECD, 2007).

The political economy of migration regulation

The non-existence of a World Migration Organisation[9] and the restrictive nature of migration policies are closely connected. Countries of immigration are loath to jettison even a small part of their sovereignty as the benefits of co-operation appear to be diffuse.

To co-operate or not to co-operate? A problem of asymmetry

The main reason for the difficulty in co-operating on migration is linked to the asymmetry of benefits between industrialised and developing countries. While trade is mainly driven by comparative advantage, migration is based on absolute advantage (Hatton, 2007).[10] In other words, firms in rich countries have a clear interest in importing foreign labour to reduce costs, while workers, who have to face such competition, are not interested in moving to poorer countries.

In this respect, Figure 2.1 shows the differences in income between the top ten countries of immigration in the North and their respective top country of origin in the South. It illustrates the asymmetry of benefits between workers from high-wage countries and those from low-wage countries. It is a matter of fact that the income per capita in the United Kingdom is almost 1 000% higher than in India, and more than 600% higher in Spain than in Morocco. This implies that by moving to India or to Morocco, workers from the UK and Spain would suffer on average an income loss of 91% and 86%, respectively. US workers moving to Mexico would lose "only" 69% of their income, on average.

The result of this asymmetry problem is twofold. At the national level, there are virtually no organised interest groups in industrialised countries willing to fight to gain access to foreign labour markets, contrary to exporters who can clearly identify an interest in accessing foreign markets. At the international level, migration-related negotiations lack an overarching common goal, namely the free movement of people. Industrialised countries do not want to commit to objectives they consider at odds with their interests, above all politically.

Moreover, countries are more likely to diverge on ideal principles of migration (and free movement) than on trade and capital. Immigrants, unlike capital goods, come with their own preferences and cultures (Gordon, 2010). It is the case that public opinion in most countries of immigration – not to say all – does not view the arrival of foreign workers favourably, and negative attitudes seem to harden as the share of immigrants in the population increases (Dustmann and Preston, 2001; Hatton, 2007).

Figure 2.1. **Income gap in main South-North migration corridors, 2009**
(current USD, PPP)

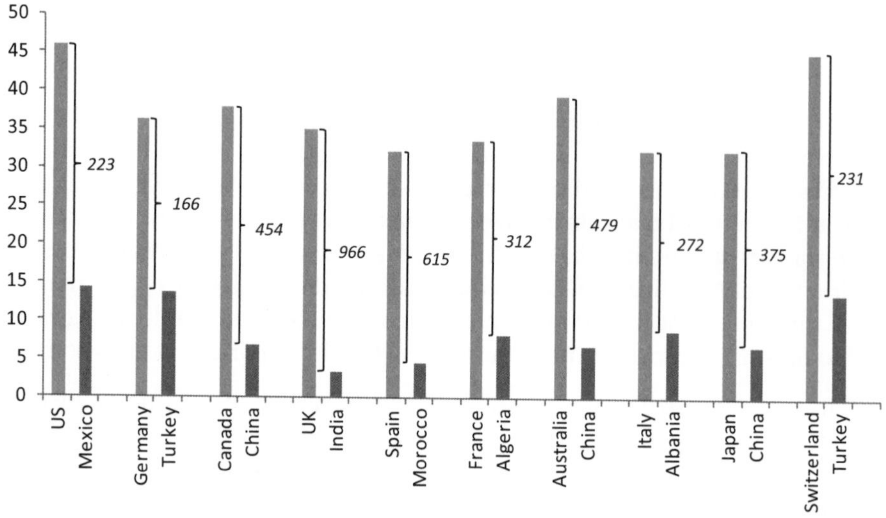

Notes: The income gap is the difference between the income per capita in countries of destination and origin. Figures represent the percentage difference of the income between countries in the South and in the North.
Source: Authors' calculations based on *World Development Indicators*, World Bank.

The reasons are both economic and non-economic. Two non-economic issues particularly worry citizens in host countries: security and national identity. The proliferation of terrorism over the last decade[11] has made Western countries more vulnerable to external threats and has led public opinion increasingly to associate immigration with insecurity. In parallel, there has been growing concern regarding the integration of immigrants, or lack of it, as illustrated by the controversy that arose in the United States following Huntington (2004)'s assertion that "the persistent inflow of Hispanic immigrants threatens to divide the United States into two peoples, two cultures, and two languages". Similarly, political leaders in Canada, Germany and the United Kingdom have recently challenged multiculturalism in their countries, while the debate on national identity in France eventually crystallised anti-immigrant opinions.

However, economic determinants seem to prevail over cultural and political factors, at least for labour market participants.[12] Using a survey on public attitudes, Mayda (2006) argues that, even though xenophobic feelings manifest themselves in anti-immigration preferences, labour market explanations of attitudes toward foreigners are not altered by non-economic variables. Native workers tend to indeed consider immigrants with similar skills as direct competitors in the labour market. Therefore, skilled individuals favour immigration when foreign workers are mostly unskilled, and oppose it as the skill composition of immigrants increases. Similarly, Benhabib (1996) shows that in equilibrium there is less immigration in more unequal countries because of its effect on the capital-labour ratio.

Hatton (2007) and O'Rourke and Sinnot (2006) show that while the interaction between education and gross domestic product (GDP) per capita is negative, the interaction between education and the Gini coefficient of household income is positive. In other words, the scarcity of skills plays a major role in attitudes on immigration. High-skilled workers feel less threatened by foreign competition in high-income than in low-income countries, and also less threatened in more equal than unequal countries. In addition, Boeri (2010) suggests that welfare systems affect the skill composition of immigrants: higher social spending comes with a lower skill content of immigration. The poorest, the unemployed and the least educated individuals are the most concerned by the fiscal implications of immigration, and they probably consider immigrants as direct competitors for social benefits.

From individual attitudes to concrete immigration policies

To explain how individual attitudes towards immigrants translate into migration policies, Facchini and Mayda (2008) contemplate two alternative political-economy models: one based on the median-voter framework, the other one on interest-group dynamics. They argue that migration outcomes are directly related to voters' preferences: the more opposed to immigration the median voter, the more restrictive migration policies are. However, migration policies continue to be relatively open if we consider the strong anti-immigrant attitude in most destination countries. One explanation is that policy makers are generally more educated and more liberal, hence less anti-immigrant than the median voter (Betts, 1988; Hansen, 2000). But no empirical evidence confirms such an assumption (Hatton and Williamson, 2005).

Another explanation is that pro-immigration interest groups offset voters' preferences by actively lobbying for more favourable legislation, while anti-immigrant groups (taxpayers, unskilled workers, xenophobes, for example) have more diffuse interests and are less successful in their lobbying efforts. Facchini *et al.* (2010) confirm the role of lobbying groups in shaping migration policy in the United States by showing that a 10% increase in lobbying expenditures per native worker by business groups is associated with a 3.1% to 5% increase in the number of visas per native worker. Conversely, a 1% increase in the union membership rate (a proxy for lobbying expenditures by labour groups) implies a 2.6% to 5.6% drop in the number of visas per native worker.

Migration policy regimes in developing countries do not differ much from the policies in industrialised countries. Restrictions on immigration are the rule: high-skilled foreign workers are more easily accepted than low-skilled migrants, and temporary flows prevail over permanent immigration (UNDP, 2009). Native workers in developing countries likely feel that immigration affects them even more directly than in industrialised countries, because of the prevalence of low-skilled labour in the composition of both the domestic and foreign workforce (which is consistent with Mayda's findings, 2006).

The fact that immigrants come from neighbouring countries does not prevent political leaders from exploiting the issue of immigration (see Chapter 3). The restrictive nature of immigration policies in developing countries has also been strengthened by European nations' growing trend to externalise their migration policies: that is, to transfer the burden of the fight against unauthorised immigration to the countries of origin and transit in exchange for financial and technical co-operation (Ndiaye and Robin, 2010).

Counterproductive effects of non-cooperative policies

The current governance of international migration flows, characterised by the lack of international co-operation and the restrictive nature of policies, is the result of a political trade-off between voters' preferences and interest group pressures. It is, however, striking that the main beneficiaries of a more open migration-policy regime, the migrants themselves, are not part of the political process in the countries of immigration, at least *ex ante* (Hatton, 2007). This does not mean that they are the only losers in the current system. In fact, migration protectionism is not intrinsically different from trade protectionism: it is a non-cooperative strategy resulting in a sub-optimal equilibrium. But what exactly are the adverse effects of restrictive migration measures?

Financial and human cost of restrictive migration policies

The costs of restrictive immigration policies are less evident than those of trade protectionism, the adverse effects of which have long been identified.[13] Yet non-cooperative migration policies generate negative externalities, not only for the countries of origin, but also for those of destination (Fernández-Huertas Moraga, 2008).

Figure 2.2 illustrates these negative externalities. Countries of origin incur a welfare loss arising from the fact that emigration cannot act as a safety valve for the labour market and that the economy receives a relatively small amount of remittances (see Chapter 4). In turn, countries of emigration have few incentives to co-operate to restrict emigration and irregular immigration tends to increase. As a result, countries of destination face high costs in enforcing immigration laws, which are eventually assumed by taxpayers.

Figure 2.2. **The negative externalities of non-cooperative migration policies**

Welfare loss

Migration
restrictions

Regular migration

Countries of
destination

Countries of
origin

Irregular migration

Countries of transit

Enforcement costs

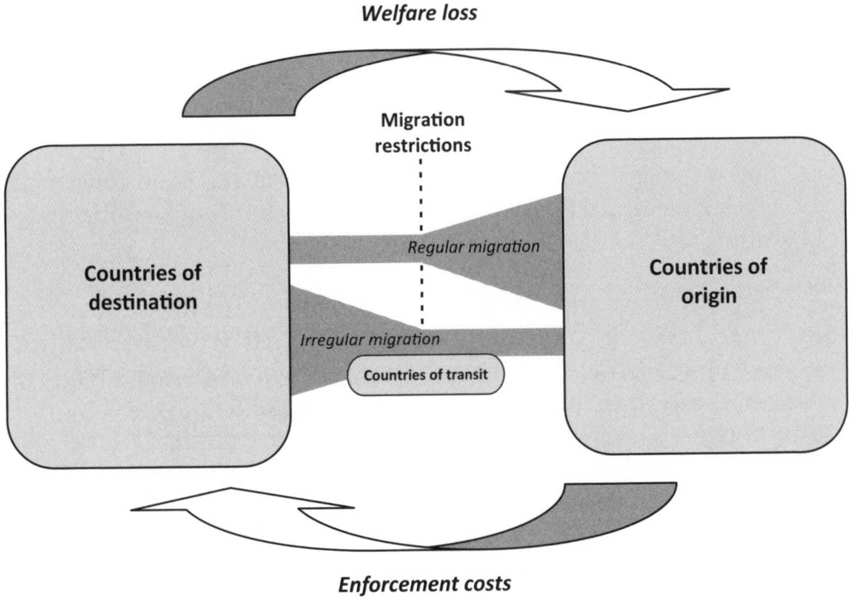

The strengthening of border controls requires a growing number of officials in charge of issuing visas, controlling entries, enforcing laws, patrolling borders, or deporting undocumented immigrants. Martin (2004) estimates that in 2002

five industrialised countries alone (Canada, Germany, the Netherlands, the United Kingdom and the United States) spent around USD 17 billion enforcing migration restrictions. Salant and Weeks (2007) argue that law enforcement activities involving unauthorised immigrants in the 24 US counties along the US-Mexico border cost around USD 192 million in 2006 (USD 1.23 billion in total between 1999 and 2006). San Diego County, by spending USD 77 million, incurred almost half of all these costs (USD 565 million over the 1999-2006 period.)

Altogether, the US spent around USD 15 billion in 2009 on border enforcement: USD 9.5 billion for US Customs and Border Protection, and USD 5.4 billion for US Immigration and Customs Enforcement (Hanson, 2009). These costs do not include deportations of immigrants to their home country. In France, a 2008 Senate Report estimated that the annual cost of expelling undocumented foreigners was about EUR 415.2 million, implying EUR 20 970 per individual (Bernard-Reymond, 2008).

In addition, several countries around the world have taken the radical decision to erect walls, not only for security-related reasons (Israel and the West Bank, India and Pakistan, South and North Korea, for example), but also, and increasingly, to control unwanted border crossings. The two most notorious cases concern the border between the United States and Mexico, and between Spain and Morocco. But they are not the only ones:

- Botswana, one of Africa's wealthiest nations, has been constructing a 500 km electrical fence at the Zimbabwean border to combat irregular immigration;

- Saudi Arabia has been doing the same at the border with Yemen to protect against the smuggling of drugs, weapons and migrants;

- India has also been fencing its entire 4 000 km border with Bangladesh, where the pressure of environmental refugees has increased.

- In Costa Rica, authorities built a 1.5 kilometre-long, 2.5 metre-high wall to try to discourage immigrants coming from Nicaragua. Federal police patrol the border in pickup trucks and boats.

And China may soon start worrying about the lack of fencing or barrier along its roughly 22 000 kilometre boundary as immigrants from poorer countries in the South begin pouring in.[14] The result is a significant rise in public expenditure arising from the construction process itself, but also from the maintenance and surveillance, sometimes with very sophisticated equipment, of these barriers (Mergier, 2009).

Restrictive immigration policies also have indirect costs, one of them being the adverse impact of migration restrictions on the tourism sector, which is affected by the policy of caution that tends to characterise visa-issuing procedures. Besides, the fight against immigration may encourage national firms to move their activities off-shore to low-wage countries, thus creating even more unemployment problems for low-skilled workers than immigration itself (Bhagwati and Blinder, 2009).

Finally, the fight against unauthorised immigration poses serious human rights issues, illustrated by the growing number of migrant deaths in the Saharan and Sonoran deserts, drownings in the Rio Grande river, or shipwrecks along the African and Mediterranean coasts. Massey (2007), for instance, shows that the death rate from suffocation, drowning, heat exhaustion or exposure during undocumented crossing of the US-Mexico border tripled between 1992 and 2002. UNITED, a European network supporting migrants and refugees, has documented more than 15 000 deaths related to the protectionist measures of a so-called "Fortress Europe" between January 1993 and October 2011.[15] Every country holds sovereignty over its own territory and has the right to deny entry to unwanted immigrants. But there is an argument that sovereign states should take into account the repercussions of their policies.

Costly migration policies are not always effective

The global rise of border controls has not been transformed into a reduction in international migration. On the contrary, migration flows have accelerated over the last decades, with only a slight slowdown over the last three years because of the global economic crisis (OECD, 2010). The number of unauthorised immigrants, in particular, has increased despite, or more likely because of, the tightening of border controls. As long as the gap in human development between nations remains significant, people will continue to move to the wealthiest parts of the world, no matter what the administrative or physical barriers may be.

Therefore, strict border controls tend to translate into high levels of irregular immigration. Those who succeed in circumventing the many barriers are generally not likely to return, even temporarily, for fear of not being able to enter again. In this sense, restrictive immigration-policy regimes can be likened to a "subsidy" for organised crime networks that grow richer thanks to migrant smuggling. Massey (2007) argues that the average cost of hiring a *coyote* to irregularly cross the US-Mexico border has increased from around USD 400 to approximately USD 1 200 in real terms between 1980 and 2002 (+200%).

Because of their insecure status, irregular immigrants are vulnerable to labour exploitation (and human trafficking). As a result, receiving countries are more exposed to unfair competition between the companies that employ regular workers (either native or foreign-born) and those that take advantage of the vulnerability of immigrants. The upshot of this growing underground economy is a significant loss of tax revenues for the state (Legrain, 2007). In addition, undocumented immigrants are reluctant to make long-term investments in their host countries (Hanson, 2010).

All in all, immigration policies alter the distribution of regular and irregular immigrants, but only slightly affect the overall number. In the same way, by making border crossing more difficult, policies displace migration corridors, making them more dangerous, and contribute to increasing the human cost.

But economic conditions both in sending and receiving countries, coupled with diaspora networks, play a more significant role in the international movement of people than migration policies themselves. Migration flows began to slow down by the beginning of the global economic crisis, and not as a direct consequence of the increase in immigration barriers (OECD, 2009b). In reality the closing of borders in times of prosperity has a small impact on the entry of foreign workers attracted by the economic opportunities they know to exist. By contrast, when the economic situation worsens, restrictive policies tend to become oversized and would-be migrants unwilling to move to countries in recession.

Introducing the benefits of immigration in the debate

While immigration is a hotly contested issue in both media and political arenas, there is more of a consensus among economists on the benefits it yields:

- Foreign workers help relieve sectors suffering from labour shortages and solve mismatching problems on the labour market, hence contributing to strengthening labour supply and competitiveness;

- High-skilled immigrants generate positive output in terms of total factor productivity, but also in terms of research, development and innovation;

- The settlement of immigrants also benefits population-sensitive sectors, such as housing, transport and urban infrastructure, and gives rise to a cumulative causation process,[16] which helps firms generate economies of scale (Romer, 1996).

- Since workers are consumers too, immigration enables the expansion of the domestic market and spurs aggregate demand;

- As immigrant stocks grow in a country, they eventually become vectors for trade with their home country;

- Foreign workers contribute to the financing of social protection and pay-as-you-go pension systems, and make it possible to solve, at least partly, demographic imbalances between active and inactive populations (Chojnicki and Ragot, 2011).

But evidence-based results are rarely mentioned in the political debate, where immigration occupies a disproportionate amount of space, and which tends to focus on the costs of the phenomenon. As explained earlier, issues such as employment, wages, social protection, security[17] and cultural integration particularly worry citizens of migrant-receiving countries. In this respect, it would be valuable to understand why political leaders do not introduce the positive effects of immigration into the debate, at least to partially mitigate anti-immigration attitudes within society. In fact, "the planned reforms of migration policies need to involve a radical effort to enhance public knowledge and understanding of migration, notably regarding its economic, social and cultural impact" in order to "resist the temptation to exploit this issue for political ends" (OECD, 2010).

Public authorities also have a role to play in minimising the perceived costs of immigration by adopting a comprehensive set of policies aiming at a better integration of immigrants in society (see Chapter 3). A more flexible regulation of international migration flows, within a co-operative framework, would also enable a reduction of the costs of restrictive immigration policies and would contribute to better match the international supply and demand of labour. The report will develop these ideas in Chapter 5.

Notes

1. Even though integration policies are strongly connected to the regulation of flows and the migration-development nexus (see Chapter 5), they concern more the local, national and even regional governance levels than the global one.

2. ILO Conventions are available at: www.ilo.org/ilolex/english/convdisp1.htm.

3. Available at: www2.ohchr.org/english/law/cmw.htm.

4. Legge 15 luglio 2009, n. 94.

5. Arizona SB 1070.

6. The next UN High-level Dialogue on Migration and Development will take place in 2013.

7. The French Ministry of Immigration, Integration, National Identity and Mutually Supportive Development (*Développement solidaire*), which was created in May 2007 after the election of Nicolas Sarkozy as president, was absorbed in February 2011 by the Ministry of the Interior, now in charge of migration issues.

8. Although the concept of co-development is generally associated with migration, it can also include other issues related to North-South relations, such as fair trade, responsible tourism or environment (sustainable co-development).

9. The idea of a WMO was in particular proposed by Bhagwati (2003) and Helton (2003).

10. Hatton argues that real wage gaps between rich and poor countries are due to differences in overall total factor productivity, not in relative factor endowments (which is the case for trade). Therefore, the incentive to migrate depends on absolute rather than on comparative advantage.

11. Symbolised by the 9 September 2001 New York attacks and the 7 July 2005 London bombings.

12. O'Rourke and Sinnott (2006) find that non-economic factors are more important for individuals not in the labour force. It is indeed easier to set up side payments for labour market participants, for instance social safety nets and training programmes, than for the rest of the population (see Chapter 5).

13. Trade protectionism implies, no matter the choice of policy instrument (tariffs, subsidies, quotas, for example), higher prices for consumers and lower productivity levels.

14. "Illegal immigrants pour across border seeking work", *Los Angeles Times*, 19 September, 2010.

15. "Fortress Europe" refers to the different European immigration policies that are liable to endanger migrant lives, such as stricter asylum laws, border militarisation, detention camps, or still deportation. For more details, see: www.unitedagainstracism.org/pages/campfatalrealities.htm.

16. A rapid population growth implies a strong demand for current consumption goods, housing and infrastructure, which, in turn, leads to an increase in labour demand. This "cumulative causation" contributes to the rapid and self-sustained development of urban areas (Krugman, 1991).

17. Wadsworth (2010) argues that contrary to the traditional belief that immigration increases insecurity, US cities with the largest growth in the proportion of immigrant population between 1990 and 2000 experienced larger decreases in homicide and robbery rates.

References

AidWatch (2010), *Penalty against Poverty: More and Better EU Aid Can Score Millennium Development Goals*, Concord AidWatch Initiative.

Baldwin R. and S. Evenett (2009), *The Collapse of Global Trade, Murky Protectionism, and the Crisis: Recommendations for the G20*, CEPR, London.

Benhabib, J. (1996), "On the Political Economy of Immigration", *European Economic Review*, Vol.40, pp.1737-1743.

Bernard-Reymon, P. (2008), *Rapport général n°99 (2008-2009)*, fait au nom de la Commission des Finances, Sénat, Paris.

Berthélemy, J.C., M. Beuran and M. Maurel (2009), "Aid and Migration: Substitutes or Complements?" *World Development*, Vol. 37, No. 10, pp. 1589-1599.

Betts, K. (1988), *Ideology and Immigration: Australia, 1976-1987*, Melbourne University Press, Melbourne.

Bhagwati, J. (2003), "Borders beyond Control", *Foreign Affairs*, Vol. 82, No. 1, pp. 98-104.

Bhagwati, J. and A. Blinder (2009), *Offshoring of American Jobs: What Response from US Economic Policy?*, Massachusetts Institute of Technology, Cambridge, MA.

Boeri, T. (2010), "Immigration to the Land of redistribution", *Economica, Vol. 77*, No. 4, pp. 651-687.

Böhning, W.R. (1994), "Helping Migrants to Stay at Home", *Annals of the American Academy of Political and Social Science*, Vol. 534, No. 1, pp. 165-177.

Chamie, J. and B. Mirkin (2010), "Calls Mount Everywhere for Deportation of Illegal Immigrants", Yale Global Online, Yale Center for the Study of Globalization.

Chojnicki, X. and L. Ragot (2011), "Immigration, vieillissement démographique et financement de la protection sociale : une évaluation par l'équilibre général calculable appliqué à la France", *CEPII Working Paper*, No. 13, CEPII Paris.

Daum, C. (1998), "Développement des pays d'origine et flux migratoires: la nécessaire déconnexion", *Hommes et Migrations*, Vol. 1214, pp. 58-72.

DUSTMANN, C. and I. PRESTON (2001), "Attitudes to Ethnic Minorities: Ethnic Context and Location Decisions", *Economic Journal* Vol, 111, No. 470, pp. 353-373.

FACCHINI, G. and A.M. MAYDA (2008), "From Individual Attitudes Towards Migrants to Migration Policy Outcomes: Theory and Evidence", *Economic Policy*, Vol. 23, No. 56, pp. 651-713.

FACCHINI, G., A.M. MAYDA and P. MISHRA (2010), "Do Interest Groups Affect US Immigration Policy?", *CReAM Discussion Paper* No. 04/09, Centre for Research and Analysis of Migration.

FERNÁNDEZ-HUERTAS MORAGA, J. (2008), "A General Model of Bilateral Migration Agreements", *UFAE and IAE Working Paper Series*, No. 755.08.

FLORES SÁNCHEZ, L. and L. MARTÍN RIVERO (2009), "Remesas en tiempos de crisis", *Investigación Económica*, IXE, June.

FRIEDMAN, T. (2009), "The Open-Door Bailout", *New York Times*, 11 February.

GORDON, J. (2010), "People are not Bananas: How Immigration Differs from Trade", *Northwestern University Law Review*, Vol. 104, No. 3, pp. 1109-1145.

HAAS, H. de (2007), "Turning the Tide? Why Development Will Not Stop Migration", *Development and Change*, Vol. 38, No. 5, pp. 819-841.

HANSEN, R. (2000), *Citizenship and Immigration in Postwar Britain: The Institutional Origins of a Multicultural Nation*, Oxford University Press, Oxford.

HANSON, G. (2009), *The Economics and Policy of Illegal Immigration in the United States*. Migration Policy Institute, Washington, DC.

HANSON, G. (2010), "The Governance of Migration Policy", *Journal of Human Development and Capabilities*, Vol. 11, No. 2, pp. 185-207.

HATTON, T. (2007), "Should We Have a WTO for International Migration?" *Economic Policy*, Vol. 22, No. 50, pp. 339-383.

HATTON, T. and J. WILLIAMSON (2005), *Global Migration and the World Economy: Two Centuries of Policy and Performance*, MIT Press, Cambridge, MA.

HELTON, A. (2003), "People Movement: The Need for a World Migration Organisation", Posted on www.opendemocracy.net, 1 May.

HUNTINGTON, S. (2004), "The Hispanic Challenge", *Foreign Policy*, March/April.

KHOUDOUR-CASTÉRAS, D. (2009), "Les migrants au cœur de la tourmente économique", *L'économie mondiale 2010*, CEPII, La Découverte, Paris, pp. 93-106.

KHOUDOUR-CASTÉRAS, D. (2010), "Les enjeux de la politique française de développement solidaire", *Regards croisés sur l'économie*, Vol. 8, pp. 190-198.

KRUGMAN, P. (1991), *Geography and Trade*, MIT Press, Cambridge, MA.

LEGRAIN, P. (2007), *Immigrants: Your Country Needs Them*, Abacus, London.

MALGESINI, G. (2001), "Reflexiones sobre migración, cooperación y desarrollo", *Arxius de Ciencies Socials* 5, pp. 123-146.

MARTIN, P. (2004), "Migration", in *Global Crises, Global Solutions*, LOMBORG, B., ed. Cambridge University Press, Cambridge, pp. 443-477.

MARTIN, P., S. MARTIN and S. CROSS (2007), "High-level Dialogue on Migration and Development", *International Migration*, Vol. 45, No. 1, pp. 7-25.

MASSEY, D. (2007), "When Less is More: Border Enforcement and Undocumented Migration", Testimony before the Subcommittee on Immigration, Citizenship, Refugees, Border Security, and International Law. Committee on the Judiciary US House of Representatives, Washington, DC.

MAYDA, A.M. (2006), "Who Is Against Immigration? A Cross-country Investigation of Individual Attitudes Toward Immigrants", *Review of Economics and Statistics*, Vol. 88, No. 3, pp. 510-530.

MERGIER, A.M. (2009), "Los otros muros", *Proceso*, 9 November.

NAÏR, S. (1997), *Rapport de bilan et d'orientation sur la politique de codéveloppement liée aux flux migratoires*, Premier Ministre, Paris.

NDIAYE, M. and N. ROBIN (2010), "Les migrations internationales en Afrique de l'Ouest: Une dynamique de régionalisation articulée à la mondialisation", *IMI Working Paper* 23.

OECD (2004), *Trade and Migration: Building Bridges for Global Labour Mobility*, OECD, Paris.

OECD (2007), *Policy Coherence for Development: Migration and Developing Countries*, OECD, Paris.

OECD (2008), "West African Mobility and Migration Policies of OECD Countries", *West African Studies*, OECD, Paris.

OECD (2009a), *Government at a Glance 2009*, OECD, Paris.

OECD (2009b), *International Migration Outlook 2009*, OECD, Paris.

OECD (2010), *International Migration Outlook 2010*, OECD, Paris.

O'ROURKE, K. and R. SINNOTT (2006), "The Determinants of Individual Attitudes toward Immigration", *European Journal of Political Economy*, Vol. 22, No. 4, pp. 838-861.

ROMER, P. (1996), "Why Indeed in America? Theory, History, and the Origins of Modern Economic Growth", *American Economic Review*, Vol. 86, No. 2, pp. 202-206.

SALANT, T. and J. WEEKS (2007), *Undocumented Immigrants in US-Mexico Border Counties: The Costs of Law Enforcement and Criminal Justice Services*, US/Mexico Border Counties Coalition, University of Arizona.

UN Secretary-General (2007), *International Migration and Development*. Report for the 63rd session of the UN General Assembly, United Nations, New York, NY.

UNDP (2009), *Human Development Report 2009. Overcoming Barriers: Human Mobility and Development*, UNDP, Palgrave Macmillan, New York, NY.

WADSWORTH, T. (2010), "Is Immigration Responsible for the Crime Drop? An Assessment of the Influence of Immigration on Changes in Violent Crime Between 1990 and 2000", *Social Science Quarterly*, Vol. 91, No. 2, pp. 531-553.

WEIL, P. (2002), "Towards a Coherent Policy of Co-Development", *International Migration* Vol. 40, No. 3, pp. 41-56.

Chapter 3

Immigrant integration in the South

Abstract

Although South-South migrants face much of the same resentment from the locally born over jobs and wages as their South-North counterparts, the issues in South-South flows need to be analysed from a quite different standpoint. Whereas Northern receiving countries tend to be relatively homogenous in terms of language, culture and ethnicity, this is often not the case in the fractionalised and multi-ethnic countries of the South where borders are porous and immigration controls lax. An examination of immigrant experience in West Africa and in particular Ghana shows that governments do not give priority to integration, and Northern models of assimilation and multiculturalism are not necessarily applicable. Lack of integration can lead to the formation of ghettos with associated acute poverty and disease. The problems of refugees and stranded migrants add an extra dimension to the issues of social cohesion and integration.

The changing geography of economic growth has been accompanied by a marked shift in global wealth (OECD, 2010). The world's economic centre of gravity has moved both eastwards and southwards, and developing countries are playing an increasing role in international governance. Channels of interaction between developing countries have become busier, especially in respect of South-South trade and factor mobility. Migration between developing countries[1] has also significantly increased and diversified over the last two decades. South-South migration stocks currently outnumber the stocks between South and North, and they are likely to keep rising in the future, not only because migration policies in developed economies are increasingly restrictive, but also because fast-growing economies in the South represent new magnets for potential migrants.

As the number of immigrants in developing countries has risen, problems related to discrimination and integration have surfaced in tandem. As in the relatively richer countries of the North where there is a longer tradition of immigration policy, local populations seldom perceive the arrival and settlement of foreign workers favourably. Low-skilled immigrants, in particular, are often blamed for taking jobs away from locals and applying downward pressure on their wages and bargaining power (see Chapter 4). Foreigners then serve as scapegoats for the economic problems of the country – above all when there is not much of a social safety net in place. They are held responsible for the rise of unemployment and insecurity, and in extreme cases can be victims of anti-immigrant riots, such as those occurring in South Africa in 2008.

However, integration issues in the South need to be analysed from a different angle from that in the South-North context, especially if the many other challenges that governments have on their agendas are considered. First, socio-economic characteristics, of both countries of destination and (self-selected) immigrants, are different, as are the problems faced by the latter. Second, the notion itself of integration is challenged in most countries of immigration, whatever the "model" in place – assimilation or multiculturalism (Simon, 2011). But this does not mean that developing countries should not tackle integration issues. In fact, the non-integration of immigrants may be more costly than in the North when tensions spiral out of control.

This chapter relies heavily on the experience of West Africa and primarily on the results of two workshops (one in Dakar, the other in Accra) and interviews with experts, immigrants, non-governmental and international organisations, policy makers and private businesses in Ghana in 2010[2] to analyse how the experience of immigrants in the South is different from that of those in the North. West Africa is an interesting region in which to study immigrant integration as it boasts the highest levels of (growing) intra-regional migration in the world. These labour movements present an economic opportunity for the region but also a potential threat to social cohesion. In one of the most extreme cases of non-integration, Côte d'Ivoire erupted into civil war. Finally, the wide diversity of economies in the region makes migration a natural part of the regional economic process.

This chapter argues that although most migrants from the South are found in the South, immigrant integration is not a current priority for many policy makers in developing countries. However, discrimination and the tendency of immigrants to live in makeshift communities help breed divisions in society and generate economic and social costs. Because migration is highly circular, labour activities are mostly informal, and relative deprivation between locals and immigrants may appear negligible. Analysing immigrant integration in the South therefore requires a different approach from analysis in the North.

South-South migration: is social cohesion at risk?

The global eastward and southward shift in wealth especially in the 2000s has contributed to modifying the geography of international migration. The drop in the cost of international transport, the improvement and accessibility of information and telecommunication technologies, and the income growth in many fast-growing economies have combined to reduce the financial constraints required to emigrate, thus enabling potential migrants to move to more distant destinations and in greater numbers. In this changing geography, South-South migration is due to occupy a prominent place. Apart from the major oil exporters, which have traditionally attracted foreign workers, new industrialising countries have become centres of labour attraction.

Shifting wealth, shifting migration flows

Migration flows are dominated by a few major corridors (Table 3.1). With almost 12 million Mexican migrants living in the United States, the Mexico-US corridor is the largest. But most top corridors (11 out of 20) concern South-South migration, mainly in Asia, while only two corridors correspond to North-North migration (Puerto Rico to the United States, and the United Kingdom to Australia). India is involved in six of these corridors either as a country of origin (in three cases to other developing countries, in one case to a developed economy) or as a country of destination (in two cases).

Table 3.1. **Top 20 migration corridors (excluding transition economies), 2010**
millions of migrants

	South-South flows		South-North flows		North-North Flows	
1			Mexico → US	11.6		
2	Bangladesh → India	3.3				
3			Turkey → Germany	2.7		
4	China → Hong Kong, China	2.2				
5	India → United Arab Emirates	2.2				
6			China → US	1.7		
7			Philippines → US	1.7		
8	Afghanistan → Iran	1.7				
9			India → US	1.7		
10					Puerto Rico → US	1.7
11	West Bank and Gaza → Syria	1.5				
12	India → Saudi Arabia	1.5				
13	Indonesia → Malaysia	1.4				
14	Burkina Faso → Côte d'Ivoire	1.3				
15					UK → Australia	1.2
16			Viet Nam → US	1.2		
17	Pakistan → India	1.2				
18			El Salvador → US	1.1		
19	Malaysia → Singapore	1.1				
20	India → Bangladesh	1.1				

Note: Main corridors in transition economies are Russia-Ukraine (3.7 million migrants), Ukraine-Russia (3.6 million), Kazakhstan-Russia (2.6 million), and Russia-Kazakhstan (2.2 million).
Source: World Bank (2010).

A growing number of developing countries receive more immigrants than they send. Table 3.2 classifies net immigration countries in the South according to their income group and their speed of growth.[3] The income level of receiving countries does not seem to play a prevalent role here, since 40% of the countries of net immigration are low-income economies (14 out of 36). By contrast, the rate of growth matters, as 29 of the net recipients in the South are classified as either affluent or converging economies (*i.e.* high income countries or those with a per capita growth rate over the decade twice that of OECD rates). This confirms that beyond the wage gap between countries, migrants are attracted by current job prospects.

Table 3.2 also includes sectoral categories such as major manufactured goods and oil exporters. In this respect, labour demand for oil production is a significant driver of South-South migration. Saudi Arabia and the United Arab Emirates, for instance, have many more immigrants (7.3 million and 3.3 million, respectively, in 2010) than emigrants (187 700 and 55 900), and the foreign population amounts up to 70% of the labour force in some Gulf countries. Altogether, 8 out of 37 net immigration countries are major oil exporters, 5 of them being both high-income and affluent economies. Exporters of manufactured goods, such as Hong Kong, China and Singapore, also attract foreign workers, although not in the same proportion as oil producers.

Table 3.2. **Main net immigration countries in the South, 2010**

Income group / 4-speed world	High	Middle	Low
Affluent	Bahrain (O) Brunei (O) Hong Kong, China* (M) Kuwait* (O) Macao Oman (O) Singapore* (M) Saudi Arabia* (O) UAE* (O)		
Converging	Argentina Venezuela (O)	Botswana Costa Rica Iran (O, R) Jordan* (R) Lebanon (R) Malaysia (M) Maldives Namibia South Africa* Syria* (O, R) Thailand (M)	Chad (R) Djibouti (R) Gambia Ghana* Nepal Nigeria (O) Rwanda Tanzania (R)
Struggling		Gabon (O)	Côte d'Ivoire*
Poor			Comoros Kenya (R) Malawi Solomon Islands Zambia (R)

Notes: * Top ten net immigration countries (in volume); (M): major manufactured goods exporters (manufactured products represent more than 50% of total exports); (O): major oil exporters (oil represents more than 50% of total exports); (R): major asylum countries (refugees represent more than 20% of immigrants).

Sources: The four-speed-world classification comes from OECD (2010); income groups, oil and manufactured goods exporters correspond to categories coined by the UNCTAD (2010); migration and refugees data come from World Bank (2010).

The fact that South-South migration outnumbers South-North stocks does not mean that going to another developing country is always the first choice of migrants from the South. In many cases, the choice is not theirs to make. Administrative barriers in developed countries are so high, even for high-skilled workers, that most would-be migrants have no other option than to try their luck in other developing countries. In addition, the financial cost of moving to distant richer countries prevents most candidates from the South from doing so (de Haas, 2011; Martin and Taylor, 1996). This explains why South-South migration often corresponds to movements between poor countries.

As shown in Figure 3.1, while emigrants from middle and high-income countries mainly move to developed economies, migrants from low-income developing countries have a developing country as their first destination. In 26 out of 40 cases, the first destination is another low-income country.

Figure 3.1. **First destination of migrants from developing countries** by income group, 2005

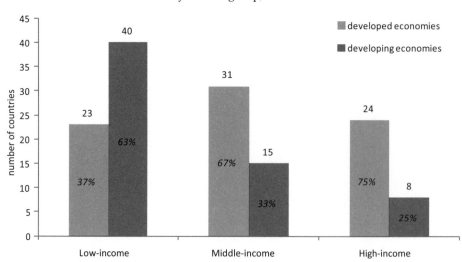

Source: Authors' calculations based on Ratha and Shaw (2007).

Why immigrant integration matters

Despite the growing importance of South-South migration, many developing countries do not consider integration a priority.[4] Yet, ignoring integration comes with a cost, one that is ignored until problems become insuperable and there is a political backlash in reaction. The lack of integration policies is often reinforced by discriminatory practices, both official and hidden. The high concentration of refugees and migrants stuck in transit in the South contributes to increasing the vulnerability of migrants and the socio-economic costs faced by the "host" society.

Non-integration and political backlash in the South

By nature immigration implies pressure on social cohesion. In general immigrants are perceived negatively by the locally born, as individuals taking something away, without giving back. They are viewed as putting pressure on society and draining resources, all the while acting in their own interests, sometimes as groups. This makes scapegoating easy for policy makers eager to win favour with voters. Immigrants are thus often held responsible for all that ails in society and eventually, without proper policy, such situations incite riots, attacks and civil conflict.

Official discriminatory practice can come in different forms – some more apparent and destructive than others. In 2004, for instance, Côte d'Ivoire passed a law that essentially gave Ivoirians priority over foreigners in all types of jobs, from qualified to manual labour.[5] Likewise, Sierra Leone's constitution authorises discrimination against "non-native" citizens (Chua, 2003).[6]

Discrimination can materialise in the form of lower wages and barred access to jobs, housing and services. In its most extreme forms, it may be synonymous with human trafficking and labour exploitation. Human Rights Watch (2010), for instance, reported severe abuse of labour rights in the case of migrant workers from Cambodia, Laos and Myanmar in Thailand. It also condemned the incapacity – and unwillingness – of local authorities to investigate complaints related to the exploitation of labour. Similarly, in 2005 the UN Committee on the Elimination of Racial Discrimination condemned the Nigerian government for "active discrimination by people who consider themselves as the original inhabitants to their region against settlers from other States".[7] Nigerian constitutional guarantees against racial discrimination do not, in fact, extend to non-citizens (CLO, 2005).

Religion also forms a core determinant of discrimination. Many Gulf countries, for instance, bar freedom of religious expression, which in particular affects Christian Filipino immigrants working in the oil industry or as domestic workers. In West Africa, Muslims in Côte d'Ivoire, Ghana, Liberia and Nigeria have claimed to feel discriminated against on several levels, while Christians allege discrimination in Guinea, (USDoS, 2010a). The types of discrimination range from citizenship and voting rights in Côte d'Ivoire, employment access in Nigeria to political and social exclusion in Ghana. In some cases, official discriminatory behaviour puts immigrants in difficult positions.[8]

The lack of integration does not only affect immigrants. Many people gain when immigrants are successfully integrated, and everyone loses when they are not.[9] As ghettos develop, for instance, they tend to become increasingly exclusive as a result of a grouped protective measure against xenophobic attacks (see Box 3.1). They also deal a major blow to the natural environment and eventually become nests of extreme poverty, even as the country gets richer. Because these enclaves are characterised by very primitive levels of sanitation, they act as vectors for drug-resistant and deadly diseases, such as influenza pandemics, tuberculosis and HIV/AIDS (UN-Habitat, 2010). In addition, without schools and medical clinics, human capital development, and thus social and intergenerational mobility, are halted.

Pockets of extreme poverty not only breed disease and circular poverty traps but also growing negative sentiments towards host native workers and government. There is a risk that the social contract erodes while organised crime and popular forms of justice develop. As the degree of infringement of local laws and customs by immigrants rises, costs also increase for the receiving country in providing more administrative services (*e.g.* police) to maintain order. In many cases these tensions escalate to violence. In some cases, ethnic and racial tensions can even generate civil unrest and long-term political instability, as in Côte d'Ivoire.

Failure to integrate immigrants can have an element of wider contagion: it can induce immigrants to go back (or be forced back) to their countries of origin and spread conflict. For instance, migratory movements were partially to blame for the expansion and length of the conflict in the late 1990s: conflict in Rwanda quickly engendered local fighting in Angola, Burundi, the Democratic Republic of Congo and Uganda.

Box 3.1. **Finding refuge in migrant ghettos: the case of Old Fadama, Accra**

Resentment and opposition can force immigrants to seek or create enclaves of poverty-stricken ghettos, which in turn make it easier to discriminate against them. Slum-dwellers comprise three main groups (not mutually exclusive): the poor and uneducated, women and immigrants. The plight of living in slums is to be excluded from "the right to vote, the right to enter and enjoy all areas of the city, the right to use social and cultural facilities and venues, the right to access basic services, and various other rights which effectively restrict their full enjoyment of the right to the city." (UN-Habitat, 2010).

Why do immigrants crowd together if it exposes them to finger-pointing? First, there is an aspect of familiarity. Migrants may not want to venture into the unknown and rather seek a certain level of comfort. Second, local perceptions against immigrants lead to stereotyping and eventually to discrimination. Within enclaves, immigrants have a greater chance of being treated as equals or continue living within their pre-established social hierarchies. Third, enclaves may enable immigrants without legal documentation to live and stay in the country while being sheltered from authority. Immigrants may feel safer if those around them are also without required "papers". Conversely, they may feel that within an immigrant enclave they can blend more easily into a larger group where there is a mix of regular and irregular workers.

Accra's well-known Old Fadama settlement constitutes a good illustration of the problem. Nicknamed "Sodom and Gomorrah" (or more formally "Agbogbloshie"), Old Fadama is like a world in itself, made up of diasporas from all over Ghana and other West African countries. It is a highly stigmatised place. But although it may appear chaotic to municipality officials, it is very organised, with its own rules and regulations. This type of setting is common in many informal settlements across West Africa. Makoko in Lagos and West Point in Liberia also exist in parallel with the world outside.

However, residents of Old Fadama suffer poor sanitation, and women are vulnerable to sexual predators and disease – the settlement lies in a region prone to flooding. Education services are rare. Many immigrants are temporary residents (so children are often not resident long enough to settle) and make return trips home to visit, to help at harvest time, or to try to start a business venture. Most work in the informal economy, particularly making and selling foodstuffs (Pellow, 2011; Tufuor, 2009).

Unfortunately for many of these workers and residents, Old Fadama also sits in the way of government plans which by 2009 took a firm decision to evict the more than 40 000 dwellers without any form of compensation or relocation. While many immigrants have since been evicted, a constant battle over the right to keep their homes has garnered support from other communities, including some outside of Ghana. The community has since moved to building networks across Accra of community-based and non-governmental organisations (NGOs) with a scope which goes beyond the prevention of the Old Fadama evictions to addressing broader issues of social exclusion faced by Ghana's urban poor. But the looming threat of eviction remains.

Particular cases of vulnerability: refugees and stranded migrants

The high concentration of refugees and migrants stuck in transit in the South contributes to increasing the vulnerability of migrants and the socio-economic costs faced by the "host" society.

Refugees are especially vulnerable as conflict and immigration have a relatively Southern face, clearly noticeable following the repercussions of the drought in the Horn of Africa (see Chapter 1). While the worldwide stock of refugees (16.3 million in 2010) amounts to 7.6% of total migration flows, refugees in developing countries (11.1 million) represent 13.8% of total immigrants (World Bank, 2010). In 2010 more than 4.4 million refugees, representing 42% of the world's total, lived in countries whose GDP per capita was below USD 3 000 (UNHCR, 2011). When this is viewed in relative terms to the size of national resources (number of refugees for each US dollar of per capita GDP), the first 24 countries in the world are developing countries. Germany, the 25th in this list, is the first developed country. Pakistan is home to 710 refugees using this measure; Germany 17 (Figure 3.2).

Figure 3.2. **Number of refugees per USD 1 GDP (PPP) per capita, 2010**

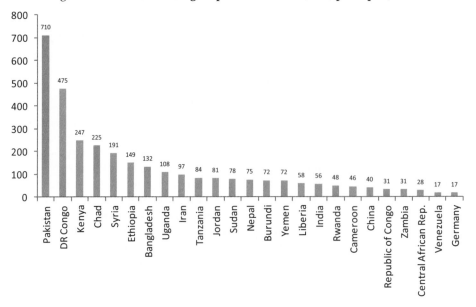

Note: Figures represent the number of refugees for each US dollar of its per capita GDP.
Source: UNHCR (2011), *Global Trends 2010.*

The UNHCR is the primary international authority on decisions made for refugees; it is also responsible for their temporary and long-term integration. While refugees are provided with access to health care, education and specific skills-training, they often also arrive in a hostile environment. Xenophobia arises naturally because nationals see the new arrivals obtaining special treatment from the United Nations. The fact that the UNHCR normally organises refugees in camps facilitates the formation of enclaves, thus limiting the possibilities of social inclusion. National governments also intervene in the integration of refugees. For instance, the Benin government has allowed Togolese refugees to attend school in the country, following civil conflict in Togo in 2005 (USDoS, 2010b).

Stranded migrants en route to Europe form a particular group at risk of human rights violations (UNHCR, 2010). Since 2000 a major anti-immigrant backlash in Libya has contributed to a diversification of trans-Saharan migration routes and an increasing presence of immigrants in other North African countries (de Haas, 2007; Hamood, 2006). But reliable figures on transit migrants are hard to come by.

Bensaâd (2003) reported that in 2003, the city of Agadez in Niger recorded a minimum of 65 000 transit migrants heading north. In fact, Niger is increasingly becoming a major point of convergence for many immigrants going to Libya and Algeria, either to stay or continue on to Europe. One of the reasons is that the government has taken a very open position in its approach to the Economic Community of West African States (ECOWAS) protocol on free movement (OECD, 2009a). For this reason, the International Organization for Migration (IOM) recently opened two migrant transit and assistance centres, in Dirkou (on the route to/from Libya) and Assamaka (on the route to/from Algeria).[10] The 2011 Libyan crisis has clearly dampened the prospects associated with migrating to Libya. A Reuters report estimates that over 200 000 migrants have returned home to Niger and that billions of CFA francs have been lost in trade and remittances since conflict erupted in February 2011.[11]

In addition to being victims of xenophobia as well as racial and ethnic discrimination, the irregular status of immigrants in transit countries subjects them to a wide range of abuse committed not only by smugglers and human traffickers, but also by border guards, immigration and police officers, and local people. Violations include extortion and exploitation, arbitrary detention in inhumane conditions, lack of due process, deprivation of access to basic services and physical abuse and harassment.[12] Unaccompanied children and women are the primary victims, a direct consequence of the feminisation of migration. In this respect, the lack of access to social networks and legal aid services increases the risks of being forced into commercial sex activity, contracting sexually transmitted infections and incurring unwanted pregnancies.

How can immigrants be better integrated in the South, particularly with the added difficulties of hidden and official discrimination and the particular cases of refugees and stranded migrants? Turning to traditional models of integration, notably those dominating the debate in the North, may not be the optimal solution. Instead, a new organic integration model, taking into account the realities of the labour market and the general makeup of the South should be developed.

Why traditional models of integration do not apply in the South

As pointed out by Sadiq (2009), the global understanding of citizenship is based "overwhelmingly on the states of Western Europe and North America. In these states the government's power to regulate entry and settlement is unquestioned." The same can be said of immigrant integration. The notion of integration that most policy makers understand is relatively concrete, one where immigrants stay permanently, learn the language and eventually their measurable socio-economic statuses (wages, types of jobs, education, school quality, consumer goods) converge to match those of the locally born.

In this respect, Figure 3.3 displays a 2x2 typology of integration models based on two cornerstones of societal living: links with members of the community of origin (in the country of immigration) and incorporation into the host society.

Figure 3.3. **A typology of integration models**

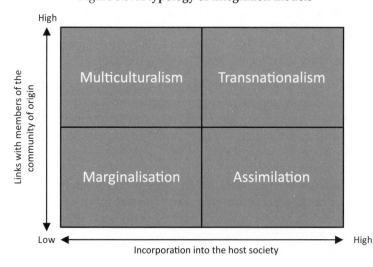

Marginalisation is frequent both in the North and the South. It occurs when immigrants fail to integrate into the host society at the same time as they break links with fellow-countrymen. This is precisely the situation that leads to increased vulnerability and generates high costs for society.

At the other end is **transnationalism**, which refers to immigrants perfectly incorporated into the host society, while also maintaining strong links with their community of origin, both in sending and receiving countries. Transnationalism is a growing theme for migration research in the North (Guarnizo, 2003; IMISCOE, 2010; Østergaard-Nielsen, 2003). But even though the idea behind transnationalism has existed for centuries, especially in the South where seasonal circular migration constitutes a lifestyle, it is an ideal type whose conditions are difficult to fulfil.

The two other cases correspond to intermediate situations, but also to two very different models of integration, which dominate discussions in the North. In the assimilation model, a significant degree of cultural adaptation by immigrants is assumed. In the multiculturalism approach, the capacity of a community to structure collective life prevails. The multicultural character of society is alleged to be reinforced by mutual understanding between various sub-communities in the country. But neither really fits the realities of the South.

Limits of the assimilation model

Models that aim for the assimilation of immigrants, as in continental Europe, are not very adapted to societies in the South, for two reasons. First, migration from nearby countries is more prevalent in the South (neighbourhood effect) and second, the overall economic and social climate is often dire for both migrants and the locally born (low relative deprivation).

Neighbourhood effect

Despite the gradual global fall in the reliance on language and colonial ties, migration within the South still relies primarily on physical proximity. It is a fact that South-South migration stocks between neighbouring countries are more prevalent than between South and North. Forty-five out of 63 developing countries (71%) whose emigrants have as their first destination another developing country share a border with that country. Mexico is the only developing country (out of 78) sharing a border with the first country of destination of its emigrants, namely the United States, when that country is developed. Even though transport costs are falling worldwide, a solid land border affords easier travel and lower opportunity costs.

In addition, the formalities for entering a country are easier to circumvent or simply ignore in many countries of the South than in the North; what is regulatory and legal in the South is not necessarily reflected in reality. Governments are overburdened with other priorities, which means that, with a limited administrative capacity, immigration controls are often overlooked. In cases where that issue is indeed dealt with, it is usually and increasingly done under the pretext of national security concerns. This has direct implications for integration. As a large amount of labour movements in the South can be attributed to short-term movements to areas where borders are often left unmonitored, the migratory system in this sense is smooth and seamless – and pro-cyclical with the demand for labour.

The neighbourhood effect means it is easier not only to emigrate but also to integrate into another country. [13] In fact, cultural and linguistic ties play a primary role, particularly for lower-skilled (and temporary) immigrants. Bengali speakers from Bangladesh favour neighbourhoods in Delhi where they can find people speaking their language. Similarly, the Ewe from Togo seek work in the eastern regions of Ghana, where Ewe is the primary language, a factor that facilitates their seasonal migration for work in the cocoa plantations. Some languages have even evolved as primary migratory route languages, joining people with similar customs across large spaces. Such is the case with the Hausa language and the Islamic faith, facilitating trade relations in West Africa for centuries. These ties go beyond language: religion, food, working habits and family customs all help in forming immigration routes (Amor *et al.*, 2010).

These examples demonstrate that it is not necessarily the ability to speak the country's national language that facilitates migration and integration. Bengali is a recognised official language in parts of India, but not in Delhi. In Ghana the national language is English while in Togo it is French. Hausa is a recognised national language in only two countries (Niger and Nigeria) despite its wide use across West Africa, and even beyond. International borders split groups with similar languages and cultures, and the migratory links that continue to bind them after decades, sometimes centuries, are international in nature.

Low relative deprivation

In many developing countries, local people often do not have access to formal employment, decent housing or social protection. At the same time, the absence of a comprehensive welfare state in many developing countries lowers economic and social discrepancies between foreign-born and local-born populations and makes integration less central.

One significant example is related to informality. Despite the rise in the number of multinational companies in the South, the few high-quality jobs that have been created are often filled through international recruiting (OECD, 2009b). The lack of formal job creation by the private sector means that it has a smaller role to play in the integration of new workers than it normally has in the North. The high prevalence of informality in the South (over 50%) implies that job insecurity affects individuals, whether they are immigrants or not.

One consequence of this lack of formal jobs is that the absence of a welfare state affects equally both immigrants and local workers: when economic shocks hit the country, both suffer from the lack of a social safety net. For instance, as China has little social safety net to speak of, there is little resentment of the many Vietnamese immigrants entering the country using public services.[14]

Differentiating between regular and irregular immigrants, even on basic civil rights, may thus be largely futile in the South. Indeed, immigrants are disproportionately represented in the informal sector (Amin, 2010; De Vreyer *et al.*, 2009 for examples in West Africa), because of the type of channels they use to enter the country, the sectors they work in, and the low administrative capacity of the destination country properly to register them. Because the informal sector helps them blend into society, authorities often have little capacity to count and manage their inflow. In many countries, identification cards do not even exist for the locally born, let alone immigrants, although change is under way in several countries.[15]

What, therefore, is regarded as a lack of integration in the North is the normal condition of most citizens in the South.[16]

Limits of the multiculturalism model

The "multiculturalism" model, popular in Anglo-Saxon countries, is also not adapted to the challenges faced by migrant-receiving countries in the South. Many developing countries already display a great diversity of backgrounds. First, the geographic diversity implies that immigrants face very different challenges according to the country in which they settle. Even within countries, geographic and demographic differences are considerable. The dichotomy between rural and urban settlements, coupled with the population density in migrant-receiving areas, is particularly significant in terms of immigrant integration. The low level of national economic integration in many countries means that many regions operate semi-autonomously; regional cultures thus dominate in economic, social, cultural and even legal aspects.

Moreover, and even if the neighbouring effect means that cultures are somewhat similar, most societies in the South already exhibit high levels of cultural diversity. Even if the Ewe and Akan share relatively similar habits compared to the Jat and Bengalis, it does not mean their habits are not different (and *vice versa*, in India). Based on pure ethnicity, the South is in general more diverse – but cultures between migrants and locally born populations are relatively closer.

Cultural diversity is a consequence of the geographic diversity of the South. Even though a significant share of migration from Southern countries consists of intra-regional flows, cultural differences between countries of origin and destination remain significant. In particular, the diversification of flows in the last years implies growing cultural differences between immigrants and native populations, which may deter integration (as discussed in various contexts and regions in Amor *et al.*, 2010; Lucassen, 2005; Ozyurt, 2009). In these circumstances relying on a model with the objective of facilitating the ethnic character of many communities may simply be aiming for the *status quo* – and not necessarily be helping integration.

As an illustration, Figures 3.4 and 3.5 show ethnic and linguistic fractionalisation in a number of OECD countries in comparison with West Africa.[17] Both indicate a much higher prevalence of diversity in West Africa. Even in countries considered very multi-ethnic, such as the United States and Belgium, diversity is lower than in West Africa.

Figure 3.4. **Ethnic fractionalisation by country, OECD vs. West Africa**

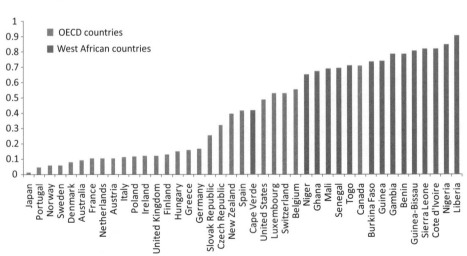

Figure 3.5. **Linguistic fractionalisation by country, OECD vs. West Africa**

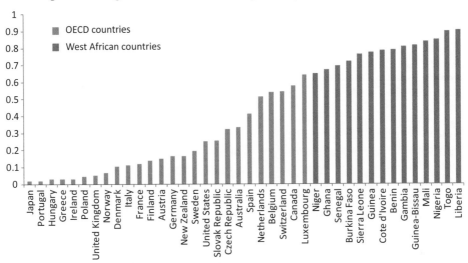

Note: for Figures 3.4 and 3.5: The fractionalisation data set measures the degree of ethnic (racial characteristics), linguistic and religious heterogeneity in various countries (only linguistic and ethnic are shown). The higher the index, the more fractionalised are the countries. In most cases the primary source is national censuses, and often based on subjective judgement. Information on how the index is compiled and issues of comparability are explained in Alesina *et al.* (2010).
Source: Alesina *et al.* (2003), revised in 2010.

This has important repercussions for integration, which might be more connected to internal fractionalisation than nationality. Continuing with the example of West Africa, immigration within the region is perhaps more part of the greater urbanisation process unfolding in developing countries; or at least to a certain extent. In 1960 urban population accounted for around 15% of the West African population; it was about 44% in 2005 (OECD, 2009a). As borders and ethnic lines are not congruent in West Africa, internal and international and migration are often part of the same process: rural Malians and Senegalese moving to Dakar, rural Beninois and Nigerians moving to Lagos.

Discrimination against new members of society may in this case not be the same as discrimination against foreigners. In some cases international migrants are more easily integrated than internal migrants as part of the same process of urbanisation. Good examples of this phenomenon are found in the SKBo region[18] and the "mega-region" running from Accra to Ibadan, through Lagos (Dahou *et al.*, 2002; UN-Habitat, 2010). A survey conducted by UN-Habitat in 2009 found differences in responses on social exclusion in seven different African cities were nearly the same for international immigrants and rural migrants (Figure 3.6).

Figure 3.6. **Perceived degree of exclusion of underprivileged groups**
(seven African cities)

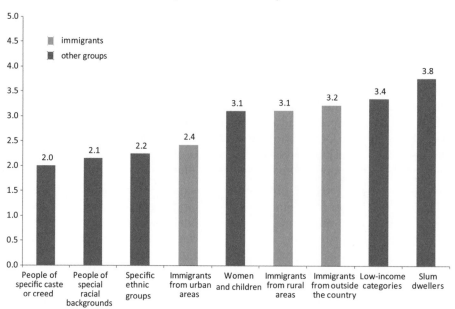

Note: Average of ratings (on a scale of 0 to 5, 5 being high perceived exclusion) by local experts responding to the UN-HABITAT 2009 survey in seven African cities (Abuja, Accra, Dakar, Ibadan, Johannesburg, Mombasa, Nairobi).
Source: UN-HABITAT (2010).

Under these circumstances, defining and measuring immigrant integration become much more difficult (see Box 3.2). Integration in West Africa has much more to do with human rights, attitudes and perceptions, often in very hidden forms, than with the formal right on paper to be protected or the economic convergence of immigrants. The neighbouring effect and multi-ethnic makeup of the South obscure many of the problems of integration, because on the one hand new members of society have a culture which is close to that of the locally born. Yet on the other there are so many of these small groups that society is extremely multi-ethnic. Moreover, the mere fact that they are labelled migrants provides the authorities with the opportunity to blame all that ails in society on them, with little political repercussion.

Box 3.2. How can we measure integration in the South?

Measures of integration in the North are hardly applicable in the South. First, legal benchmarking indices, such as they are practised in Europe, are less relevant than in the North because laws and regulations are not enforced. Measuring whether discrimination is a crime punishable by law or not between countries is futile if the legal system is burdensome, inefficient or nearly non-existent. Second, many of the outcomes measured for the integration of immigrants in the North are simply not applicable in the South because they are based on economic and social outcomes that are also less likely to be achieved by the locally born. Trying to measure whether immigrants have access to the formal job market might not be useful in many cases, particularly when 80% of the population are informally employed.

Studies need rather to focus on different measures of discrimination, reflecting the field realities of the country – services and benefits easily accessible to most of the local population. This can be done, for example, by focusing on a very flexible, yet realistic, definition of wages and employment, and by comparing the wages of informal working immigrants in a specific sector with those of their local counterparts. The key lies in identifying the more comparable counterpart. Although it costs more, experimental testing can also help in revealing whether subtle discrimination exists (see the experiment by Bossuroy and Selway (2011) in Chennai, India as an example).

Because not only immigrants, but also the poorest locally born, live in large, informal slums, studies also need to focus on measures of segregation, that is, turning to the sociological concept of spatial analysis as a measure of integration (Lee, 2009). For instance, in cities where slums are the norm for a large part of the population, an important way to measure immigrant integration is by observing the spatial component of city living arrangements as between locals and immigrants over time. Attempting simply to measure outcomes may not reveal the true driving force behind non-integration – it may be that segregation between the two groups in different ghettos is contributing to non-integration.

But objective data are clearly not enough. Subjective questions in surveys, such as attitude towards immigrants or degree of acceptance in society, may be the easiest and quickest way to reveal, and even predict, whether discrimination and conflict pose a problem. Periodic views on integration and acceptance in the community, on immigration and on work and life satisfaction would help determine the likely non-linear relationship between immigration and integration outcomes (see, for instance, Fertig, 2004, or Maxwell, 2010).

What priorities?

Because locals face many of the same difficulties as immigrants, it would probably be a mistake to formulate a policy framework exclusively oriented towards immigrants. Indeed, how can public authorities provide immigrants with services not even available to their own citizens? Expecting successful integration of immigrants in a number of areas considered luxuries even for locals may be unattainable, and to a certain degree undesirable for fear of resentment from locals. Main economic, social and political reforms should then be universal in nature, and focus on priority areas such as employment, social protection and education.

But universal reforms, although desirable, may also generate several adverse effects in terms of integration. There is a risk that governments may decide to give priority to their own citizens, thus excluding immigrants from economic and social benefits. And even if reforms cover foreign populations, it is likely that undocumented immigrants may not be included. Yet, because borders in many developing countries are so porous, irregular migration is the norm, not the exception. Undocumented immigrants may therefore find themselves more isolated than before, above all if reforms come with the generalisation of identification systems.

To avoid major risks of marginalisation, and the associated costs for society, public authorities in developing countries need to adopt specific measures to protect the basic rights of immigrants, in particular the most vulnerable. In this respect, the case of stranded migrants requires a specific treatment so that the burden is not only shouldered by transit countries, but also by those of origin and final – or originally intended – destination. In addition, measures to fight discrimination must be implemented.

But even though protecting migrant rights and fighting discrimination are crucial, integration also implies that immigrants are better incorporated into the host society. Chapter 5 will show, based on the experience of various developing countries, that such goals can be achieved.

Annex 3.A1. Research work in Ghana

Background work was done in preparation for this chapter in 2010 in Ghana, one of the main countries of immigration in West Africa (both in absolute and relative terms). The first purpose was to investigate policies and programmes that facilitate the integration of immigrants and help fight discrimination in countries of the South. A second aim was to uncover attitudes with respect to immigrants and immigration policy from diverse points of views.

The integration of immigrants in Ghana is an interesting aspect of South-South migration, as immigration to Ghana from neighbouring West African countries is significant and increasing. In the last decade, the Ghanaian government has reformed its immigration system, ratified the UN Convention on Migrants' Rights and modernised its immigration control technology. In addition, migrant hometown associations (HTAs) and private sector initiatives have been developing quickly in response to the increase in immigration.

The authors held a one-day experts meeting at the University of Ghana (Accra) and carried out interviews with academics; policy makers; international organisations and NGOs; the private sector and trade unions; and immigrants and their representatives. Each interview, as well as the workshop, was based on the following core questions:

1. What is the current state of immigration in Ghana?

2. What are the different dimensions of immigrant integration in Ghana?

3. What policies foster integration in Ghana and what are their limits?

4. How can the situation be improved for both immigrants and the locally born?

In addition, individual interviews focused on subjective questions, asking respondents how they felt about the state of immigrant integration in Ghana. Respondents were asked general questions but encouraged to give long and detailed answers. The additional questions were as follows:

According to you [...]

1. [...] what is the state of immigrant integration in Ghana?

   a. Are immigrants well integrated in Ghana?

   b. Is it an important policy issue? Should the government spend money on integration?

   c. What rights should immigrants have in Ghana? What rights should they not have?

   d. Do immigrants contribute positively or negatively to the economy? Should Ghana open the borders to more immigrants?

2. [...] what determines an immigrant's successful integration?

   a. What helps an immigrant's integration?

   b. What deters it?

3. [...] does the government help in the integration of immigrants?

   a. Should it have a role? Should it do more? Less?

   b. What role should it have?

   c. Should the government protect the locally born from immigrants in matters of employment?

4. [...] whose responsibility is it to integrate immigrants?

   a. Local or national decision makers?

   b. Private businesses?

   c. Traditional leaders?

   d. International organisations? Aid donors?

5. [...] are immigrants perceived as a threat to the locally born?

   a. Are immigrants discriminated against? In what way?

   b. Is tension high between the locally born and immigrants?

Notes

1. In this chapter, "South" and "developing countries" are used interchangeably.

2. The questionnaire for the interviews is included in Annex 3.A1.

3. Based on Wolfensohn (2007), OECD (2010) develops a "four-speed" world concept, dividing countries designated as affluent (high-income countries), converging (countries catching up to the living standards of the affluent), struggling (countries facing a middle-income "glass ceiling"), and poor (under the weight of extreme poverty).

4. As one interviewee in Ghana put it, "because they are in the minority, the topic is not a priority for the government". In fact, the tendency has been to put more resources into controlling borders and irregular immigrants. In Costa Rica, for instance, a regularisation drive of irregular migrants was followed by harsher penalties in 2011 for those trying to follow in their footsteps. Fines were set for immigrants overstaying their visas, it became harder to get residency by marrying a Costa Rican and raising the financial requirement necessary for residency. New criminal rules were also put into place against immigrant smuggling.

5. Decision 1437 of 19 February 2004.

6. Section 27 of the constitution states that "no person shall be discriminated against by a law-enforcing agent or public officer or person in public authority" but an additional clause (b) adds that "the right does not apply with respect to persons who are not Sierra Leoneans or those who acquire citizenship of Sierra Leone by registration, by naturalisation or by resolution of parliament".

7. www.fidh.org, "Racial Discrimination in Nigeria: a UN committee denounces the inertia of the Nigerian government".

8. Discriminatory practices against immigrants came up in many interviews, such as "Immigrants contribute mostly positively to the economy, but not necessarily legally. Immigrants would register a business under a Ghanaian name and contribute positively, but it's illegal to run that business". Without registration, immigrants are automatically barred from most services.

9. As pointed out in interviews, for instance, "migrants from Burkina Faso are often highly welcome in Ghana because of their hard work" and "migrants contribute

positively to the Ghanaian economy by establishing businesses and creating opportunities for employment".

10. While many migrants cross intermediate countries in route to another country, a rising phenomenon is that of migrants staying in the transit countries and taking advantage of the flow of people coming through. Their impact on local economies can be considerable. In Agadez for instance, economic and cultural spillovers are being enjoyed by emerging transit cities. The city is being transformed by the new dynamic and lucrative transit migration sector: hotels, food, networks, all being exploited by the many individuals choosing to stay rather than move on (Amadou *et al.* 2009).

11. Reuters, 2 July 2011, "Libyan crisis hammering Niger economy".

12. In August and September 2010, an estimated 600 to 700 immigrants were arrested during police raids in Morocco and left deep in the desert near the Algerian border (Touzenis, 2010).

13. In general, respondents answered that integration was not a problem for immigrants in Ghana, giving answers such as "immigrants are hardly noticed and treated differently in Ghana", "some immigrants move in quietly without any problems" and "the government should be responsible for all people". Some even expressed that "with time refugees are socially and economically integrated into Ghanaian society. Some of the Liberian refugees are still in Ghana as workers and are married to Ghanaians." Even though they may be mostly in irregular situations, as one respondent put it, "immigrants in Ghana are not really integrated formally since it is difficult to get your papers straight, but nevertheless it is easy to blend in, especially if you are black".

14. "Illegal immigrants pour across border seeking work", *Los Angeles Times*, 19 September 2010.

15. Although some countries in the South, such as Ghana, India, Mexico and South Africa, are currently spending millions on such identification systems, it is not clear whether this will help or deter the integration of immigrants. These programmes usually have an enormous implementation cost since they include expensive anti-counterfeiting mechanisms such as biometric technology, including fingerprints and optical security features.

16. That is until relative deprivation between the two groups spreads. One respondent answered that "some immigrants end up taking jobs that Ghanaians should be entitled to, using Ghanaian facilities but paying their taxes in their home countries, or engaging in criminal activities in Ghana," and "the government needs to set out clear rules to ensure that immigrants do not compete unfavourably against poor Ghanaians and do not have access to more/better facilities than Ghanaians. In many responses, caution was exercised in stating that immigrants are welcome as long as they obey the rules, in answers such as "immigrants are integrated as long as they respect the rules and regulations of the host community"; "unless a crime is committed, they have no problems

living in any part of Ghana"; and "tension occurs if a crime is committed or if the immigrant appears to have some form of upper hand over the locals". One respondent answered that some immigrants contribute economically to the country, while others "also engage in negative practices like the drug trade and illegal mining activities thereby damaging the environment."

17. The average of ethnic and linguistic fractionalisation is, respectively, 0.24 and 0.23 in OECD countries, as against 0.73 and 0.75 in West Africa.

18. SKBo is the acronym given to the region comprising the cities of Sikasso (Mali), Korhogo (Côte d'Ivoire) and Bobo Dioulasso (Burkina Faso).

References

ALESINA, A., A. DEVLEESCHAUWER, W. EASTERLY and S. KURLAT (2010), "Fractionalization," *Journal of Economic Growth*, Vol. 8, No. 2, pp. 155-194.

AMADOU B., F. Boyer and H. MOUNKAILA (2009), "Le Niger, espace d'émigration et de transit vers le sud et le nord du Sahara : rôle et comportement des acteurs, recompositions spatiales et transformations socio-économiques", in *Document de synthèse des projets du programme FSP 2003-74: migrations internationales, recompositions territoriales et développement*, pp. 109-120.

AMIN, M. (2010), "Immigrants in the Informal Sector: Evidence from Africa", mimeo, available at: http://works.bepress.com/mohammad_amin/25.

AMOR, H., A. BAALI, O. OUIRARI and A. LAASSAKRI (2010), "Mode de vie, habitudes alimentaires et identité des immigrants sénégalais au Maroc", presented at the African Migration Workshop, Dakar, November 2010.

BENSAÂD, A. (2003), "Agadez, carrefour migratoire sahélo-maghrébin", *REMI*, Vol. 19, No. 1.

BOSSUROY, T. and J. SELWAY (2011), "Social Divisions and Interpersonal Transfers in India". Paper prepared for the OECD conference on Social Cohesion and Development in Paris, January.

CHUA, A. (2003), "World on Fire: How exporting free-market democracies breeds ethnic hatred and global stability", William Heinemann, London.

CLO (2005), "Status of the Implementation of International Convention on the Elimination of All Forms of Racial Discrimination in Nigeria: an Alternative Report", Civil Liberties Organisation, 67th Session of the Committee on the Elimination of Racial Discrimination, Lagos.

DAHOU, K., T. DAHOU and C. GUEYE (2002), "Espaces Frontières et Intégration Régionale: Le cas 'SKBo'", ENDA, Dakar.

FERTIG, M. (2004), "The Societal Integration of Immigrants in Germany", *IZA Discussion Paper* No. 1213, Bonn.

GUARNIZO, L. E. (2003), "The Economics of Transnational Living", *International Migration Review*, Vol. 37, No. 3, pp. 666-699.

Haas, H. de (2007), "The Myth of Invasion: Irregular Migration from West Africa to the Maghreb and the European Union", IMI Research Report.

Haas, H. de (2011), "Migration Transitions: a theoretical and empirical inquiry into the developmental drivers of international migration", *IMI Working Paper No. 24*.

Hamood, S. (2006), "African Transit Migration through Libya to Europe: The Human Cost", FMRS, AUC, Cairo.

Human Rights Watch (2010), *From the Tiger to the Crocodile: Abuse of Migrant Workers in Thailand*, Human Rights Watch, New York, NY.

IMISCOE (International Migration, Integration, and Social Cohesion) (2010), "Migration in a Globalised World, New Research Issues and Prospects", Amsterdam University Press.

Lee, C. (2009), "Sociological Theories of Immigration: Pathways to Integration for US Immigrants", *Journal of Human Behavior in the Social Environment*, Vol. 19, No. 6, pp.730-744.

Lucassen, L. (2005), "The Immigrant Threat: The Integration of Old and New Migrants in Western Europe since 1850", University of Illinois Press.

Martin, P. and J.E. Taylor (1996), "The Anatomy of a Migration Hump", in Taylor, J.E. (ed.), *Development Strategy, Employment and Migration: Insights from Models*, OECD, Paris, pp. 43-62.

Maxwell, R. (2010), "Evaluating Migrant Integration: Political Attitudes across Generations in Europe", *International Migration Review*, Vol.44, No. 1, pp.25-52.

OECD (2009a), *Atlas régional de l'Afrique de l'Ouest,* Club du Sahel et de l'Afrique de l'Ouest, OECD, Paris.

OECD (2009b), *Is Informal Normal? Towards More and better Jobs in Developing Countries,* OECD, Paris.

OECD (2010), *Perspectives on Global Development 2010: Shifting Wealth,* OECD, Paris.

Ozyurt, S. (2009), "Islam in Non-Muslim Spaces: How Religiosity of Muslim Immigrant Women Affect their Cultural and Civic Integration in Western Host Societies", The Center for Comparative Immigration Studies, UC-San Diego.

Østergaard-Nielsen, E. (2003), "The Politics of Migrants' Transnational Political Practices", *International Migration Review*, Vol. 37, No. 3, pp. 760–786.

Pellow, D. (2011), "Internal transmigrants: A Dagomba diaspora", *American Ethnologist*, Vol. 38, No. 1.

Ratha, D. and W. Shaw (2007), "South-South Migration and Remittances", *World Bank Working Paper,* No. 102, World Bank, Washington, DC.

Sadiq, K. (2009), "Paper Citizens: How Illegal Immigrants Acquire Citizenship in Developing Countries", Oxford University Press.

SIMON, P. (2011), "Benchmarking integration: Who, what and how", Ninth Coordination Meeting on International Migration, Population Division, Department of Economic and Social Affairs, United Nations, New York, NY, 17-18 February 2011.

TOUZENIS, K. (2010), "Trafficking in Human Beings", UNESCO Migration Studies 3, Paris.

TUFUOR, T. (2009), "Gender and Women Housing Problems in Accra – The Case of Old Fadama", Ghana Ministry of Water Resources Works and Housing.

UNCTAD (2010), *UNCTAD Handbook of Statistics*, United Nations, New York, NY, and Geneva.

UN-Habitat (United Nations Human Settlements Programme) (2010), "State of the World's Cities 2010/2011: Bridging the Urban Divide", UN-Habitat, Nairobi.

UNHCR (2010), "Building partnerships for identifying, protecting, assisting and resolving the situation of stranded and vulnerable migrants", Global Migration Group Practitioners' Symposium, United Nations, Geneva, 27-28 May.

UNHCR (2011), "UNHCR Global Trends 2010", UNHCR, Geneva.

USDoS (United States Departement of State) (2010a), "International Religious Freedom Report 2010", USDoS, Washington, DC.

USDoS (2010b), "Human Rights Report 2010", USDoS, Washington, DC.

VREYER, P. DE, F. GUBERT and F. ROUBAUD (2009), "Migration, Self-Selection and Returns to Education in the WAEMU", Open Access publications from Université Paris-Dauphine.

WOLFENSOHN, J. (2007), "The Four Circles of a Changing World", *International Herald Tribune*, 4 June.

WORLD BANK (2008), *Migration and Remittances Factbook 2008*, World Bank, Washington, DC.

WORLD BANK (2010), *Migration and Remittances Factbook 2011*, World Bank, Washington, DC.

Chapter 4

Emigration, labour markets and development

Abstract

Migration is a major factor in development and economic convergence. It can produce substantial consequent changes in labour markets at home and in social conditions, including wage levels, household welfare, food security, child welfare and the role of women as workers and carers. Migrants' remittances can also have impacts on work, productivity and education. The level of remittances appears to be closely related to economic conditions in host countries. It is not only the households of migrants, male or female, that are affected: there are impacts on those not sending migrants. Migration seems to have a positive effect on income, production and spending on education. The relationship between "lost labour" and remittances is one that merits further study.

Chapter 2 concluded that over the last 20 years immigration has become a key and contentious topic in most industrialised countries. The financial crisis, the Arab Spring and widespread famine in East Africa have combined to reinforce this phenomenon and have highlighted the trend of retreating from the idea of more open borders. A core reason for this is tied to the perceived impact of immigration on wages and unemployment and that is, without a doubt, at the heart of academic and political debate. Some researchers argue that it contributes to an increase in unemployment and exercises downward pressure on real wages (for instance Chiswick, 2009), a fact that is vigorously disputed by others (for instance Card, 2009).

But migration has a mirror effect: it helps alleviate poverty in the migrant's home country. In this respect, more recent political consideration has been given to migration as a possible channel of development. Most studies in this branch focus on the effects of remittances on development (OECD, 2007). But the impact of labour mobility goes far beyond remittances and even migrant households. It affects employment and job opportunities in the countries of origin and produces spillovers, or chain reaction, on other households and communities.

The increasing connection between countries and the growing reliance worldwide on migration as a vector for all types of capital mean that labour markets are at the very heart of the issue. Even though these aspects have not attracted the same level of political interest, the labour market remains arguably one of the most important facets of poverty reduction. In fact, since households from poor and middle-income countries rely heavily on income derived from employment, a change in the availability of labour or jobs implies a direct change in their welfare.

This chapter focuses on the economic development of the home country by looking at changes in the labour market induced by emigration. It presents results from three OECD working papers. On one side, Gagnon (2011) shows that the intense period of emigration from Honduras following Hurricane Mitch in 1998 increased wages, particularly those of high-skilled workers, women, rural workers and workers in the private sector. On the other, Filipski and Taylor (2011) and Wouterse (2011) add contributions by simulating policy changes in host immigration countries and observing their impact on household welfare in the home country. The first case study focuses on Mexico and Nicaragua; the second on Burkina Faso.

The chapter adds its own contribution by summarising the literature on emigration and the labour market in a coherent manner for policy making. It argues that the trade-off in the household between labour lost to emigration and increasing income from remittances implies changes in labour supply for the household members staying behind. In the aggregate, the positive impact of emigration on wages in the home country is an important dimension of development and economic convergence between poorer and richer countries. Moreover, South-North migration has a bigger impact on the welfare of source countries than South-South migration. Finally, immigration policies in the home country impact on welfare and poverty in the host country, beyond migrant households.

How emigration affects migrant households

As most migration decisions are taken within the household, the immediate and most direct impact of emigration is that it alters labour decisions within the migrant household. This implies two observable circumstances that must be dealt with: a loss of labour contribution from the departed migrant followed by an inflow of economic resources in the form of remittances.

The trade-off between lost labour and remittances

Emigration reduces the available labour force within the household, but also aggregate labour capacity in communities. In certain cases it can be detrimental, as when it entails a decline in absolute production and generates issues related to food security. On the other hand, the income from remittances has an effect on the decision to work within the household: it frees up economic constraints and consequently time, the need to exert labour and opportunities of investment.

The lost-labour effect

At the household level, emigration directly reduces the overall labour force, forcing the remaining members to change their practices or making it necessary for them to supply labour. For a similar level of living standard to be maintained, the forgone production of the departed member must be replaced. The greater the migrants' previous contribution to the household, the more costly the loss of their labour becomes for the unit. For instance, if the primary breadwinner emigrates, the household faces the challenge of producing without the central component of its production unit.

Unsurprisingly, in households already living at subsistence levels, there are critical consequences. Household members, both men and women, young and old, exert more or less effort than they would have if the member had not left. In areas where labour markets are incomplete, in particular in rural regions, the effect is even more considerable. It may, in fact, be impossible to replace the forgone labour either internally or on the labour market; welfare in this case drops.

This is inevitably a gross generalisation, as many other factors come into play. First, the extent and even the direction of the change will depend on the departed member. What was their production level before leaving, what are their intentions, how long will they be gone, how much money will they send back? There are multiple contributions the emigrant may have made to the household before leaving, many of which are not measurable.

Analysis of this is largely missing in the literature, however, where research typically analyses migration at higher levels (between countries, at the national level, migrant *vs.* non-migrant households in the same community) rather than within the household. This usually yields results on the average migrant's characteristics, but not on the mechanisms that govern emigration decisions and the impact on those taking the decision to emigrate. Measurement is indeed difficult, because most migration decisions are made at the household level, requiring reliable and extensive data collection.

The impact of emigration is also related to the household's composition: the number of its members, its gender and dependency ratios (adult-child ratio) and its average educational level. If there are many members in the household, the opportunity cost of one departed member might be minimal. But if there are many more female members, and the departed member is male, a drop in productivity may ensue if the household had relied on this ratio for optimal production (Wouterse, 2008). If there are many children in the household, for instance, it may simply not be possible to work more, since time must also be spent in child-rearing.

The conditions in which the household finds itself will also define the impact of emigration. That is, either through the type of economic activities the members were undertaking before the emigration episode, its location (rural *vs.* urban, seasonality) or the general economic or legal climate (availability of work, administrative barriers). Depending on these factors, the impact may reach well beyond migrant households. As indicated above, in rural settings, where activities are based on agriculture, the impact may lead to food insecurity (see Box 4.1).

Box 4.1. **Emigration and food security**

The rural *vs.* urban dichotomy is fundamental in any labour market analysis as the challenges differ in each region. Rural areas represent a dual challenge for the households and communities left behind. First, because those who leave, owing to the self-selected nature of migration, are amongst the highest-valued human capital in these communities. As an example, since agricultural work is physically demanding, losing young males can entail a critical drop in production to the household. Second, because the forgone labour contribution cannot easily be replaced as well-functioning labour markets are seldom found in rural areas.

Further complicating the matter is the fact that the lack of complete labour markets is one of the primary determinants of emigration. Rural households heavily rely on labour to produce at least enough food for their personal consumption. A badly functioning labour market means that households living at subsistence levels must cope with the loss by either working more (*i.e.* more hours) or reshuffling labour roles within the household, since they do not have the option of hiring outside labour – even if that is financially feasible.

Damon (2009) offers a panel data study differentiating between the pure lost-labour effect and the remittances effect in rural El Salvador. El Salvador is an interesting case study because even the most conservative estimates based on US census data indicate that over 800 000 Salvadorans, equivalent to 12% of the country's population, currently live in the United States. The analysis shows that the lost-labour effect in fact increases on-farm labour hours for all family members and significantly decreases male off-farm labour hours – a general shift towards agricultural labour.

But beyond the household lost-labour effect, entire communities may also suffer. When many workers from the same rural community leave, those left behind face a mutual problem: an aggregate lack of labour to produce food. While emigration improves the personal food security of the migrant and perhaps their household, it is not clear what happens to agricultural communities in general. Research has investigated how internal migration has impacted on food chains and rural-urban linkages, but less so on how the loss in labour affects overall productivity. Does migration facilitate or hinder overall food security? Anecdotal evidence in Burkina Faso (Wouterse, 2011), Mali (Cissé and Daum, 2010) and Zimbabwe (Tsiko, 2009) shows that emigration can actually be the cause of food insecurity in some communities.

Food security is often argued in the opposite sense: that is, that environmental fluctuations and climate change push individuals and households to emigrate or because high international prices for non-food crops crowd out the value of food crops. But migration can also be the source of food insecurity. When enough young able-bodied men leave communities primarily based on agriculture, for instance, those remaining are often left with less productive capacity. While the negative impact first hits the immediate community concerned, in the aggregate it can encompass an entire country and drive food prices up.

There are several reasons that make the situation difficult to manage; for instance, the lack of a functioning labour market, poor infrastructure linking rural and urban areas, and the lack of access to land and the security of land tenure (ECA, 2004). But two aspects of migration make the situation less dire than it seems. First, absent migrants are not food consumers and so exert no pressure on food consumption. Second, remittances help alleviate consumption pressures and can be invested in better agricultural practices (Crush *et al.*, 2006).

Migrant households typically see emigration as an investment. If the household deliberately decides to suffer the loss of labour, it is usually because there is an economic incentive to do so: the receipt of remittances. In their own way, remittances also manage to impact on labour behaviour in the household – and beyond.

The remittance effect

Remittances help alleviate poverty through a pure income effect (Combes *et al.*, 2011), but they also affect household labour decisions. Theoretically, the net impact of remittances on labour supply is somewhat unclear because they are sent for various reasons. First, they may be sent for purely self-interested motives, in cases where remitters expect a future transfer in return, such as land inheritance (Lambert *et al.*, 2002). Second, the remitter's utility (in the economic literature sense) may be also linked with the household's utility in the home country, in which case altruism would explain the prevalence of transfers. Third, the theories behind the New Economics of Labour Migration (NELM) (Stark, 1991) argue that remittances act as an insurance mechanism and help smooth consumption in cases of idiosyncratic shocks to the household (Chami *et al.*, 2005). Gubert (2002), for instance, provides evidence that insurance (for crops) is an important motivation for remittances for agricultural households in Mali.

The empirical literature on migration and labour supply generally concludes that labour supply actually drops in migrant households. Evidence of this can be found on El Salvador (Acosta, 2007), Mexico (Airola, 2008; Amuedo-Dorantes and Pozo, 2006a), Guatemala (Funkhouser, 1992), Haiti (Jadotte, 2009), Colombia (Mora, 2010), the Philippines (Rodriguez and Tiongson, 2001) and a mix of Caribbean countries (Itzigsohn, 1995). But the drop in labour supply in migrant households may actually be an indirect effect of the poverty-reducing effect of remittances for four reasons:

1. Self-employment and micro-enterprises: remittances help households create self-employment. As many of these micro-enterprises stay small (fewer than five people), they may be considered as informal employment in the ILO definition sense[1] and the time people spend operating their own enterprises is often not properly captured in surveys. In Albania, for instance, the reduction of hours worked for wages in migrant households was directly linked to the increase in time spent in self-employment activities (Nazarani, 2009).

   Indeed, investment in micro-enterprises is an important counterpart of the lost-labour effect and a fundamental dimension of the emigration and development link. Studies on El Salvador (Acosta, 2006), the Philippines (Cabegin, 2006), Nicaragua (Funkhouser, 1992) and Mexico (Massey and Parrado, 1998; Woodruff and Zenteno, 2007) for instance, show that remittances help generate entrepreneurial activity in migrant households.

2. Unreported work: by decreasing financial constraints and increasing reservation wages (the lowest wage rate at which a worker would be willing to accept a particular type of job), remittances may lead household members to leave waged work for unreported work in the household. This type of informal employment is often not captured in standard surveys. The case of women in migrant households is discussed below.

3. Productivity: micro-enterprises help reduce the time required to work because the time needed to commute to the place of employment is shorter and also because productivity increases. In fact, many migrant households may have already been running a micro-enterprise, and the remitted capital serves rather for re-investment in the activity and increases in its productivity and efficiency. The fall in time worked may also originate in the fact that households with micro-enterprises schedule their own work time, rather than having it dictated by an employer.

Existing informal activities in agricultural households provide a good example. In these cases, remittances help make pre-existing activities more productive and capital-intensive. For example, remittances may help agricultural households evolve from producing low-yielding crops to commercial crops and eventually to raising cattle. Empirically this has been shown in Burkina Faso (Taylor and Wouterse, 2008), Pakistan (Adams, 1998), the Philippines (Yang, 2008) and the region of Southern Africa (Lucas, 1987). While these studies focus on rural agriculturally based households, higher capital-output ratios among remittance-receiving micro-enterprises were also found in Mexican cities (Woodruff and Zenteno, 2007).

4. Education: many households choose to invest their remittances in increasing human capital – in effect taking away household members from the labour market and into education, thus lowering labour supply. But the investment also has a second impact on labour exerted, through productivity. Human capital leads to more efficient time management and activities requiring less time. This is often the case for children, who because of financial constraints were obliged to work before the household's receipt of remittances, but also for adults investing in vocational training.

Remittances, therefore, help lift the credit constraints that often push poor households to overwork, take on bad jobs, substitute work for education and remain poorly productive. By doing so, they change labour behaviour in various ways: time worked, exertion made and investment for longer-term benefits. It is also important to consider the relationship between remitter and recipient. Research shows that not all household members are treated similarly and benefit from remittances in the same way (De Vreyer *et al.*, 2010). Because women are often those paying the price of financial constraints, their behaviour is particularly interesting.

A gender perspective

An important dynamic of the link between emigration and labour supply is played out at the gender level. Women left behind may be obliged to take on roles traditionally held by men, and if there are children in the household, they will be required to tend to their well-being as well as household management – quite apart from working to earn a living.

Using data on agricultural households in Burkina Faso, Wouterse (2008) argues that changes in the gender ratio (and consequently on gender roles) affect the productive efficiency of the household. For instance, if surplus male labour is shifted from agricultural work (in this study, South-South migration to Côte d'Ivoire), efficiency increases; in contrast, if the most productive men leave (in this study, South-North migration to Europe), efficiency decreases because women are moved from roles in which they were complementary to ones that are substitutes for men because of the internal shortage of labour.

Men are not the only ones who emigrate. The emigration of any spouse, male or female, usually leads to the other half of the partnership working less (see Airola, 2008; Amuedo-Dorantes and Pozo, 2006a; Hanson, 2007a and 2007b for Mexico, Acosta, 2006 and 2007 for El Salvador). But in general, women decrease their labour supply more than men when the household receives remittances. This is linked with an increase in their reservation wage, leading women to spend more time on household management and child-rearing rather than working and generating income. While women may diminish the amount of time they spend working in officially reported activities, they do increase the time spent in unreported household activities. Evidence of this phenomenon is found in Albania (Carletto and Mendola, 2009) and Moldova (Görlich *et al.*, 2007).

When their spouses leave, women may tend to take on many activities – including formal and informal work. Remittances simply allow them to give some of them up, offering a more flexible work schedule and enabling them to focus only on necessary work. Many household activities fall on women who move their time from working in the waged labour market to tending to children and also home care. Studies, for instance, have documented the fact that remittances to households with children keep women at home and induce their transition from paid work to self-employment (Cabegin, 2006 in Albania; Glinskaya and Lokshin, 2009 in Nepal). Cabegin (2006) gives the presence of young children in the household as an explanation; high household dependency ratios means the outflow of adults to emigration increases unreported work in the household in tending to childcare.

The decrease in labour supply, together with the fact that women usually become heads of households while husbands are away, often leads to a gain of relative intra-household power in favour of women as they now control household finances. A different set of social circumstances occurs however when women leave (see Box 4.2).

Box 4.2. **Care drain and family disintegration**

In what is being termed the "care drain", many women from developing countries are leaving their household behind to care for children or the elderly in richer countries (Ehrenreich and Hochschild, 2003). Several socio-economic and political factors explain this (D'Cunha, 2005; Fudge, 2010; Oishi, 2005):

- Demographic factors push more middle-class women to enter the labour market and increase the need for care-givers in both developed countries and also emerging countries in Asia and Latin America;

- Growing business competition has increased the pressure of working, making balancing work and family responsibilities difficult, as well as inducing change in family structures;

- The increasing marketisation of care in developed countries combined with the segmentation of the labour market has created a demand for migrant care workers;

- The global economy is generating a class of "new rich", in both developed and emerging countries, with the means to afford migrant domestic workers.

The growing demand for domestic helper and child care services is met through international migration of women from developing countries. Care work seems to be "women-specific": "Women are perceived as naturally imbued with the nurturing and domestic abilities needed for care-giving and domestic work" (D'Cunha, 2005). On the supply side, women, like male workers, migrate to support their families but also to realise their own aspirations.

In many cases, the impact of parental absence is negative, affecting the critical areas of health, education, social relations and family cohesion (GFMD, 2010). In particular, parental migration has a social and emotional cost on children left behind, who are likely to experience a destructured family, without a clear source of the authority, guidance and care indispensable for their emotional stability. The long-term absence of parents can also lower the educational opportunities of children left behind (Jampaklay, 2006). It is usually the poorest who are most affected by family disintegration as they do not have the financial means to move the entire household together (Ratha *et al.*, 2011).

Parental migration affects not only the family but also the community at large. First, it can engender juvenile delinquency. Children left behind seem more susceptible to risky behaviour (consumption of drugs and alcohol), teenage pregnancy and violent behaviour. Juvenile delinquency affects the entire society and weakens its social cohesion. Second, the community can be affected by social changes brought about by migration. Third, teachers and community leaders have to carry the burden of caring for the children. The aggregate impact of the care drain in countries with high rates of emigration adds to this burden: there is a lack of competent people to supervise children and the care workers who remain in the community are overloaded.

How emigration affects migrant-sending countries

When a national view is taken, the debate on migration and labour markets in the North tends to concentrate (negatively) on how the arrival of migrant workers impacts on other workers. Naturally, the focus is on the labour market wage and unemployment rate, as labour supply inherently changes with the influx of immigrants.

But the impact of emigration on the labour market adds an element that does not exist in the debate on immigration: remittances. As they constitute a feedback process from migration, remittances too affect labour markets in the home country – beyond the direct labour demand-supply effect. When emigrants leave and consequently have an effect on the entire labour market, remittances impact on the households that receive them directly – and consequently their labour supply. An interesting question is whether the household dynamic described in the first section translates to aggregate shifts of employment in the economy.

Remittances, moral hazard and unemployment

As seen earlier, remittances may decrease labour supply in the household for several reasons: a transition to informal types of employment, an increase in productivity or investment in human capital. There is yet another reason why household members may decrease their supply: leisure consumption. Because migrants do not directly observe the use of remittances, a "moral hazard" problem may develop between the remitter and the receiver(s): household members receiving remittances have an incentive to decrease their labour supply in order to remain eligible to receive future transfers. While lost labour might add pressure to work more, remittances reduce this pressure and may even lead household members not to work at all. In fact, the income effect of remittances on the reservation wage is often greater than the original cost of lost labour.

The moral hazard problem of remittances also plays an important role in the level of productivity of the household. Azam and Gubert (2005) found that in the Kayes region of Mali, the receipt of remittances led to a decrease in agricultural productivity, as remittance-receivers decreased their labour supply.

The mechanism behind remittances and labour markets explains why a simulation exercise (Decaluwé and Karam, 2008) found that the outflow of workers decreased unemployment in a simulation exercise on Morocco but why, by contrast, remittances keep unemployment high in Jamaica despite generally rising wages (Kim, 2007). Emigration decreases pressure on the labour market and thus more jobs are left in the home country for fewer people. Yet remittances, by decreasing labour supply in the households they are sent to, increase unemployment. In fact, in economic recessions, it is possible that the decrease in remittances arising from the downturn in the host country increases labour supply in the home country, and thus exacerbates problems of unemployment in the home country (see Box 4.3).

Box 4.3. Global economic crisis, remittances and unemployment

The recent global economic crisis is a good illustration of the moral hazard phenomenon. Many migrants affected by the crisis stopped sending money or at least reduced the amount remitted. As a result, remittances reduced in many developing countries, especially in 2009 (see Figure 4.1). To replace the lost income, many household members had to re-enter the labour market, hence contributing to increasing the labour supply and, eventually, unemployment, as the economy was unable to absorb the sudden inflow of jobseekers..

Figure 4.1. **Remittance flows to developing countries**

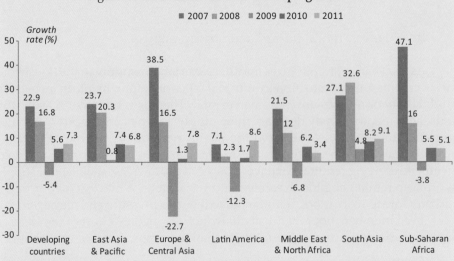

Source: Mohapatra *et al.* (2011).

Figure 4.2 features a simple correlation between changes in remittances and in unemployment, both measured as the annual growth rate (in percentage) between 2008 and 2009, for a total of 29 developing countries from Africa, Asia and Latin America. The x-axis represents changes in remittances and the y-axis the change in unemployment. The figure shows a negative correlation between the two variables (the coefficient of correlation is -0.53). In other words, the greater the drop in remittances, the higher is the increase in the unemployment rate.

Figure 4.2. **Unemployment and remittances during the global economic crisis, 2009**

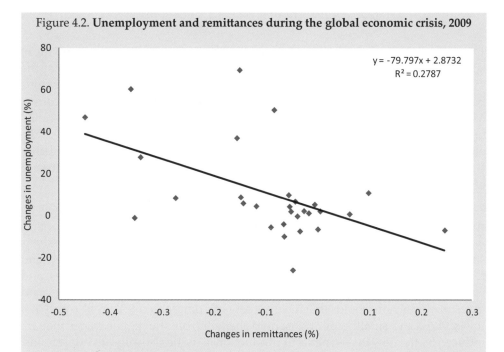

$y = -79.797x + 2.8732$
$R^2 = 0.2787$

x-axis: Changes in remittances (%)
y-axis: Changes in unemployment (%)

While not necessarily free of endogeneity problems,[2] it is an interesting correlation as it highlights the potential risk for households that rely heavily on remittances for their everyday activities. If remittances are a substitute for economic activities, they may create dependencies for households. Households that cannot or do not use remittances to create sustainable projects that generate income are bound to run into problems in times of crisis or when facing a shock, such as a positive re-evaluation of the home currency. While nothing in the table confirms causality, the relationship exposes the risks and sensitivity of a development model solely focused on migration.

A general recalibration of labour worldwide can also bring efficiencies to local labour markets. Migration regulates labour shortages and surpluses and arguably forms a natural part of the development process spurring economic and social mobility along with it. In other words, labour migration is linked to the economic convergence of poor countries to richer ones (Hatton and Williamson, 2005). In essence, the movement of workers can alter the equilibrium of the labour market.

Labour market equilibrium

Does migration change the equilibrium of the economy, and more specifically, does it have an impact on the labour market? The analysis of the macro effects of emigration can be seen in two ways: by looking at transmissions between households and by looking at aggregate macroeconomic indicators. Microeconomic models focusing on individual actors (individuals, households or firms) miss the linkages that transmit influences among households. The effects on the economic agents who are directly involved in migration are only part of the story of how migration reshapes rural economies. Direct remittance effects generally are small compared with indirect ones.

Evidence is provided by a simulation exercise by Dyer and Taylor (2009) on rural Mexican households, showing that emigration raises wages in communities where transactions are high between households. Specifically, their analysis shows that emigration tends to increase wages. Changes in labour availability and the increase in remittances impact wages and the prices of non-tradeables, and consequently generate general equilibrium effects on production, incomes and investments by households that have not sent migrants abroad. They also find that the landless and smallholder households benefit from the higher wages that are induced by the new investments in production activities by migrant households.

According to a general neoclassical labour and demand approach, a decrease in workers should lead to an increase in wages. There are two reasons for this. First, if a significant share of the economically active population leaves the country, the immediate drop in labour supply should lead to an increase in wages, at least in the short term before capital adjustment occurs. But remittances, as has been seen, also reinforce the impact if they lead to migrant household members working less, further decreasing the supply of labour – but without people actually leaving the country.

Complicating the issue slightly is the fact that workers with similar characteristics will affect each other's wages and employment chances and will follow similar market responses. The effect of complementary workers will follow in the opposite direction. In other words, there are many labour markets depending on individual skill and experience levels. For example, if many agricultural workers arrive at once, it will apply downward pressure on agricultural workers in that region, but as production increases, so will the demand for truck drivers bringing produce to the market.

The issue is still a recent and contested one for empirical economists. The link between emigration and the equilibrium of the labour market in developing countries has a few added complexities in comparison to immigration and to developing countries:

- First, as seen earlier, a number of developing countries receive large amounts of remittances, sometimes representing more than 20% of GDP (for instance Lebanon, Lesotho, Moldova and Tajikistan).

- Second, upward pressure may mount on wages and spur job creation. But, what happens in countries where certain sectors and skill levels have an immense reserve army of unemployed or under-employed?

- Third, labour market equilibria are highly influenced by the relative amount of capital and labour in the economy. Despite the benefits to labour it brings through the rebalancing of this ratio (labour becomes more scarce), the country loses since it scales down the overall labour component of its production function. That is, the overall productive capacity of the country diminishes.

The anecdotal evidence provided by Macharia (2003), on Kenya, and Ennaji and Sadiqi (2004), on Morocco, suggest that wages do increase as a result of emigration.[3] Can this be tested empirically? Several approaches can be taken to answer this question. One is to look at whether emigration contributes to wage convergence in richer countries in the long run. In historic terms, it has been argued that emigration was a contributing driver for real wage convergence to that of richer countries by helping decrease the growth of the labour force in the home country. Such was the experience, for instance, of many European countries before World War I (Boyer *et al.*, 1994; Williamson, 1996). This approach, however, requires a very long-term view. Complicating the issue is that in some countries, emigration may have also altered the structural capital-labour ratio.

Most of the recent empirical research takes inspiration from the body of work focusing on the impact of immigration, notably on Borjas (2003) and more recently extending the approach to measure the impact of emigration. In empirical terms, using an approach similar to Borjas (2003), several studies conclude that emigration did indeed increase wages in Mexico (Mishra, 2007; Aydemir and Borjas, 2007), Puerto Rico (Borjas, 2008) and Moldova (Bouton *et al.*, 2009). Using a slightly modified spatial approach to exploit regional differences in Mexico, Hanson (2007b) yields a similar conclusion.

The typical elasticity found in these studies ranges from 2% to 6% (a 10% increase in emigration leads to a 2% to 6% increase in wages). While in Hanson (2007a) it is slightly higher, his methodology does not rule out any indirect effects of emigration (the impact on growth) and therefore probably overvalues the true elasticity. A simulation exercise based on a 1998 social accounting matrix in Morocco also finds that the direction of the effect is positive (Decaluwé and Karam, 2008).

Many of these studies focus on countries that have a relatively well-functioning labour market and sustained growth. Moreover, they either look at the very long term or use historical data. What happens in countries where the labour market and economic growth are poor? Do the mechanisms work in the same way or does a reserve army of workers keep taking up the available jobs? What happens when a country is hit by a sudden shock, sending many workers away? In 1998, the track of Hurricane Mitch split Honduras in two and devastated infrastructure along its path. Economic activity ceased and many fled to the US. Box 4.4 provides the results of a study looking at the impact of emigration on Honduran wages.

Box 4.4. **Hurricane Mitch and the impact of emigration on wages in Honduras**

Honduras provides an interesting case study for the analysis of the impact of emigration on wages. In 1998, the second deadliest hurricane on record at the time swept through the country and prompted a wave of emigration. The surge in emigration was accompanied by an intense debate on its impact for the country's development, featuring campaign slogans such as "quédate con nosotros" ("stay with us") by the Honduran Association of Maquiladoras. However, while emigration may negatively have affected the maquiladora industry, it benefited Honduran workers staying behind by reducing pressures in the crowded labour market. In fact, average wages increased for workers in Honduras as a result of emigration.

To put the study in context, Honduras is a poor country with a population of fewer than 8 million inhabitants. GDP per capita is low, just over USD 4 000, somewhere in the middle of the ranking in Central America and in 2006, 60% of Honduran households were living under the national poverty line (ISACC, 2009). The labour market is highly segmented between the few existing formal jobs and the rest. Internal migration is mostly undertaken to obtain an opportunity to emigrate internationally and starting a formal business is complicated. Despite the less-than-ideal conditions in the labour market, women have increasingly entered it over the years. Until the hurricane hit, emigration from Honduras was relatively low in comparison to its neighbouring Central American countries; most movement out of the country in the 1970s and 1980s was primarily spurred by regional conflict.

According to the neoclassical model of labour, when there are many individuals with similar jobs leaving the labour market simultaneously, it experiences an upward pressure on wages. To analyse whether emigration has had an impact on wages in Honduras over the years following the hurricane, a Borjas-type of empirical framework is employed using data from bi-annual labour surveys in Honduras and partial censuses in the US for the years 2001, 2004 and 2007. The analysis shows that the sudden wave of emigration from Honduras following Hurricane Mitch yielded an increase in wages of around 10% for every 10% shift of labour supply due to emigration over these years – an elasticity much higher than the studies on other countries referenced above. But the impact diminishes over time – suggesting that capital re-adjusts to the available labour in the country, and the labour market finds its equilibrium in the long term.

The implications are interesting for policy making. As mentioned earlier, the release of pressure in a crowded labour market benefits those staying behind, even though the loss of labour decreases the overall resources available to the country. Moreover, by increasing domestic wages the country takes a step towards converging towards the economic heights of richer countries.

But what categories of workers are driving these results? Intuitively, the categories and education-experience groups with the highest emigration rates should benefit the most. This is true when education is looked at. Of four education groups, the highest emigration rates were by the highest educated followed by the lowest educated. While all education groups gained, these two groups experienced the highest gains in wages.

But it is not always necessarily the case that groups with higher emigration rates gain, for two reasons. First, categories of workers are mobile, in the sense that they can exploit job opportunities left by other categories. The rise in the number of women working in Honduras is a good example. In the study they gained much more than men, because more men were migrating. As many jobs do not necessarily discriminate between men and women, the latter were consequently left with more and better-paying jobs.

Second, the labour market is complex, and certain categories may benefit from more or less opportunity due to their intrinsic character. For instance, in the analysis above, wages in rural areas increased faster than those in urban areas, not because more rural workers left, but because incomplete labour markets imply greater difficulty in replacing workers. Similarly, workers in the private sector saw their wages rise faster than those in the public sector, not because they emigrated in higher numbers but because the (mostly) informal private sector is more reactive to economic changes than the more rigid and protected public sector.

While the emancipation of women is a good sign for development, the results above reveal potential problems in the Honduran labour market:

- First, female gains there may be more of a sign that they are taking on too much responsibility. The results hide the fact that while women have taken on a bigger economic role in society, they have not necessarily reduced other burdens.

- Second, the fact that rural areas are gaining the most means that labour markets there are highly imperfect; agricultural help is costing more because no one is left and farmers are thus losing out.

- Third, postsecondary educated workers are already those that have the highest returns to labour; an increase in their wages is only increasing inequality between skill groups. Mishra (2007) shows that emigration did indeed increase inequality between education-experience groups in Mexico from 1970 to 2000. Interestingly it is not only the most skilled that gained, however. It is the relative size of groups that matters. Being smaller than those with primary and high school education, the group with no formal education benefited the second most after the university-educated. Interestingly, many of these individuals work in the maquiladora industry, where resistance to emigration is still quite high.

Note: Based on Gagnon (2011).

The analysis cited earlier by Dyer and Taylor (2009) suggested that emigration effects transmit from migrant households to non-migrant households through economic interlinkages. Taking this analysis one step further, migration policies in other countries can impact on migrant-sending countries, and even spill over on to non-migrant households through the same mechanism. These externalities are seldom taken into account.

The international externalities of migration policies

Migration policies in countries of destination generate international externalities (see Chapter 2). Apart from a perfectly random occurrence, it is very difficult to test empirically the impact of policies. An alternative method is to construct a system of general equilibrium equations modelling household decisions and behaviour, and changing parameters to see how other parameters react. Micro-simulations have become popular in economics, these being the general intended, but also unintended, effects of policies on welfare and labour decisions.

The simulations described here are based on OECD working papers by Filipski and Taylor (2011) and Wouterse (2011). The first is based on a disaggregated rural economy-wide (DREM) framework, disaggregated by household type as well as by gender and skills, simulating changes in migration policies in the United States and Costa Rica on Mexico and Nicaragua. The second relies on a similar model of migration but simulating the impact of policy changes in Europe on Burkina Faso.

Table 4.1 displays results from a series of basic policy simulations for the corridors investigated. Details of the policies simulated are as follows. For less restrictive and more restrictive migration policies, the number of migrants in the model was increased, decreased or maintained, and other variables observed. Regularisation and exchange devaluation were tested by changing the amount of remittances that return to the migrant's household. To test the impact of a temporary migration programme, part of the migrant stock was re-allocated from a southern neighbouring country to the north (Europe).

Results are consistent with the story of this chapter. Migration in general increases income, production and expenditures in education, while decreasing labour supply – all signs of increasing welfare. Limiting migration or remittances has the opposite effect.

Table 4.1. **Immigration policies and welfare in countries of origin**

When does welfare increase?	*When does welfare decrease?*
Less restrictive policies in receiving countries	More restrictive policies in receiving countries
Temporary migration programme	Tax on remittances
Regularisation of immigrants	
Exchange rate devaluation	

Source: based on Filipski and Taylor (2011) and Wouterse (2011).

However, other interesting results warrant discussion. First, home time and labour supply are almost perfect substitutes. Second, the (positive and negative) effects on education are higher than the effects on consumption and the negative effects of a tax on remittances are higher than the positive effects of higher remittances. Overall, the positive effects of more migration are only slightly higher than the average positive effects of more remittances.

These generalised results however hide many stories that are important for well-being and for policy making. First, the destination country matters. One way to see this is to divide the simulations by South-South and South-North movements. For instance, welfare decreases for Burkina Faso households immigrating to Côte d'Ivoire. Indeed, Côte d'Ivoire is a poor country itself, albeit with many labour opportunities for work in the cocoa sector, and the income gap in comparison with Europe is large. As a result, restricting policies in the North and indirectly pushing more South-South migration decreases household welfare through opportunity costs. In the event, the largest gains are found when simulating a transfer of migrants from South-South to South-North.

However, the situation is reversed in Central America. The combination of Costa Rica being a relatively much richer country than Nicaragua and the costly trip to the US, make Costa Rica a better alternative for Nicaraguans. Welfare increases in almost every category are higher than for emigration to the US or even for Mexicans emigrating to the US. In fact, even the erosion of remittances over a five-year period still yields positive production and income effects on the household, despite their decrease or marginal increase in all other corridors.[4] The relative gap between GDP/capita in Côte d'Ivoire (USD 1 800) and Italy (USD 30 500) is simply much larger than then the gap between Costa Rica (USD 11 300) and the United States (USD 47 200).

It is also important to see who is being impacted in what way, as argued at the beginning of this chapter. For instance, the substitution between home time and labour supply suggests that it benefits women, who have less need to work outside the household. More home time means more time with children and less to devote to bad jobs. In many cases women are forced to increase their labour supply without abandoning any of the time spent at home. Women tend to prefer and benefit more from short-term and nearby emigration. South-South migration from Nicaragua to Costa Rica, for instance, benefited women more than it did men. Skill level also plays an important role. The positive effect of an increase in remittances is highest for high-skilled men and production decreases more for the low-skilled.

One final important component is the view on the long term. The positive impact of migration may take many years to play out, perhaps a generation. The simulation results shown above are a one period simulation. If instead these simulations are run over a five-year period, the results are reinforced and stronger, the positive effects of increasing migration in the long term outweighing the negative effects of remittance erosion.

Leaving the country, reshaping the labour market

Measuring the impact of emigration on labour markets in sending countries is challenging, and characterised by prevalent regional flows and high informal employment. But the challenges do not mean that no impact exists or that it is impossible to quantify it. Households with a member working abroad are subject to two contrasting forces changing over time: one linked to the loss of labour associated with the departure of the member and the other to the transfer of money benefiting the household. But migrant households are not the only ones affected by the consequences of emigration. Emigration has a national impact, notably through inherent changes in the labour force on equilibrium wages.

An improvement in statistics would facilitate more analysis, but it requires a significant effort on behalf of the policy makers in the sending country. It should also form a key objective of international co-operation, notably for the evaluation of policies. Improvement on statistics must start by integrating household surveys, as is already the case in many Asian and Latin American countries.

Many specific research questions are left unanswered and yet are important for migration policy making. First, who is it that leaves within a household? Understanding this question would help in understanding the extent of the lost-labour effect for the household. Second, what are the defining determinants between a moral hazard situation of remittances and a household investing in a micro enterprise? Third, how does the timing between the lost-labour effect and remittances impact on the household? And finally, how do remittances impact on the aggregate labour market of a country?

A better grasp of the links between emigration and labour, and more generally between migration and development, would help in a better understanding of the mechanisms at play while also facilitating a more coherent policy framework. As Chapter 5 of this report will show, this implies internalising the effects of labour policies but also their interaction with other policies, notably education, social protection and gender equality.

Notes

1. See *ILO Resolutions Concerning Statistics of Employment in the Informal Sector* adopted by the 15th International Conference of Labour Statisticians (ICLS), January 1993, as well as the following 17th Conference in 2003.

2. It is hard to argue for reverse causality since it is more typical for remittances to be sent when households face hard times. In other words, the literature points to remittances being sent when unemployment increases (a positive relationship), as an insurance (see for instance Amuedo-Dorantes and Pozo, 2006b, on Mexican migrant households). However, it is clear that both variables may be influenced by economic reasons related to the crisis; that is, unemployment rose and remittances fell because of dire economic circumstances in both home and sending countries.

3. Examples in Eastern Europe are provided by Silasi and Simina (2007) for Romania and Thaut (2009) for Lithuania.

4. Several studies show that remittances decrease proportionally to the length of stay in the countries of immigration. Funkhouser (1995) argues that remittances between the United States and Nicaragua drop by three dollars for every month spent in the US. DeSipio (2002) estimates that a 1% increase in time spent by Mexicans in the United States lowers the probability of transferring money home by 2%. Filipski and Taylor (2011) show that the annual rate of decay of remittances to Mexico is about 3.5%.

References

Acosta, P. (2006), "Labor Supply, School Attendance, and Remittances from International Migration: The case of El Salvador", *World Bank Working Paper* No. 3903, World Bank, Washington, DC.

Acosta, P. (2007), "Entrepreneurship, Labor Markets and International Remittances: Evidence from El Salvador", *International Migration Policy and Economic Development: Studies Across the Globe*, World Bank, Washington, DC.

Adams, R. (1998), "Remittances, Investment, and Rural Asset Accumulation in Pakistan", *Economic Development and Cultural Change*, Vol. 47, No. 1, pp. 155-173.

Airola, J. (2008), "Labor Supply in Response to Remittance Income: The Case of Mexico", *The Journal of Developing Areas*, Vol. 41, No. 2, pp. 69-78.

Amuedo-Dorantes, C. and S. Pozo (2006a), "Migration, Remittances, and Male and Female Employment Patterns", *American Economic Review*, American Economic Association, Vol. 96, No. 2, pp. 222-226.

Amuedo-Dorantes, C. and S. Pozo (2006b), "Remittances as insurance: evidence from Mexican immigrants", *Journal of Population Economics*, Vol. 19, No. 2, pp. 227-254.

Aydemir, A.B. and G. Borjas (2007), "A Comparative Analysis of the Labor Market Impact of International Migration: Canada, Mexico and the United States", *Journal of the European Economic Association*, Vol. 5, No. 4, pp. 663-708.

Azam, J. P. and F. Gubert (2005), "Those in Kayes. The Impact of Remittances on Their Recipients in Africa", *Revue économique*, Presses de Sciences-Po, Vol. 56, No. 6, pp. 1331-1358.

Borjas, G. (2003), "The Labor Demand Curve is Downward Sloping: Reexamining the Impact of Immigration on the Labor Market", *Quarterly Journal of Economics*, pp. 1335-1374.

Borjas, G. (2008), "Labor Outflows and Labor Inflows in Puerto Rico", *Journal of Human Capital*, University of Chicago Press, Vol. 2, No. 1, pp.32-68.

Bouton, L., S. Paul and E.R. Tiongson (2009), "The Impact of Emigration on Source Country Wages: Evidence from the Republic of Moldova", World Bank, Washington, DC, mimeo.

BOYER, G., T. HATTON and K. O'ROURKE (1994), "The Impact of Emigration on Real Wages in Ireland, 1850-1914", in HATTON & WILLIAMSON (eds.), *Migration and the International Labor Market*, 1850-1939, Routledge, New York, NY.

CABEGIN, E. (2006), "The Effect of Filipino Overseas Migration on the Non-Migrant Spouse's Market Participation and Labor Supply Behavior", *IZA Discussion Paper Series* 2240, Institute for the Study of Labor, Bonn, Germany.

CARD, D. (2009), "Immigration and Inequality", *NBER Working Paper* 14683.

CARLETTO, G. and M. MENDOLA (2009), "International Migration and Gender Differentials in the Home Labor Market: Evidence from Albania", *Development Working Papers* No. 272, Centro Studi Luca d'Agliano, University of Milano.

CHAMI, R., C. FULLENKAMP and S. JAHJAH (2005), "Are Immigrant Remittance Flows a Source of Capital for Development?", *IMF Staff Papers*, Vol. 52, No. 1, International Monetary Fund, Washington, DC.

CHISWICK, B. (2009), "Top Ten Myths and Fallacies Regarding Immigration", *IZA Policy Papers* 12, Institute for the Study of Labor (IZA), Bonn.

CISSÉ, P. and C. DAUM (2010), "Migrations internationales maliennes, recomposition des territoires migratoires et impacts sur les sociétés d'origine", in *Dynamique migratoire, migration de retour et impacts sur les sociétés d'origine au Maghreb et en Afrique de l'Ouest*, Université Mohammed V-Agdal, Rabat, Morocco, 22-23 November.

COMBES, J.L., C. EBEKE, M. MAUREL and T. YOGO (2011), "Remittances and the prevalence of working poor", *Documents de travail du Centre d'Economie de la Sorbonne* 11021, Université Panthéon-Sorbonne (Paris 1), Centre d'Economie de la Sorbonne.

CRUSH, J., B. FRAYNE and M. GRANT (2006), "Linking Migration, HIV/AIDS and Urban Food Security in Southern and Eastern Africa", International Food Policy Research Institute (IFPRI).

DAMON, A. (2009), "Household Labor Allocation in Remittance-Receiving Households: The Case of El Salvador", mimeo.

D'CUNHA, J. (2005), "Claim & Celebrate Women Migrants' Human Rights through CEDAW: The Case of Women Migrant Workers", a UNIFEM Briefing Paper, United Nations Development Fund for Women.

DECALUWÉ, B. and F. KARAM (2008), "Migration Impact on Moroccan Unemployment : a static computable general equilibrium analysis", *Documents de travail du Centre d'Economie de la Sorbonne* 08052, Université Panthéon-Sorbonne (Paris 1), Centre d'Economie de la Sorbonne.

DESIPIO, L. (2002), "Sending Money Home … for Now: Remittances and Immigrant Adaptation in the United States", in R.O. de la GARZA and B.L. LOWELL (eds.), *Sending Money Home: Hispanic Remittances and Community Development*, Rowman & Littlefield, Lanham, MD, pp. 157-87.

DYER, G. and J. E. TAYLOR (2009), "Migration and the Sending Economy: A Disaggregated Rural Economy-Wide Analysis", *The Journal of Development Studies*, Taylor and Francis Journals, Vol. 45, No. 6, pp.966-989.

ECA (2004), "Land Tenure Systems and their Impacts of Food Security and Sustainable development in Africa", Economic Commission for Africa.

EHRENREICH, B. and A. HOCHSCHILD (2003), *Global Woman: Nannies, Maids and Sex Workers in the New Economy*, Metropolitan Press, New York, NY.

ENNAJI, M. and F. SADIQI (2004), "The Impact of Male Migration from Morocco to Europe on Women: A Gender Approach", Finisterra, Vol.39, No. 77, pp.59-76.

FILIPSKI, M. and J. E. TAYLOR (2011), "The Impact of Migration Policies on Rural Household Welfare in Mexico and Nicaragua", *Working Paper* No. 298, OECD Development Centre, Paris.

FUDGE, J. (2010), "Global Care Chains: Transnational Migrant Care Workers", prepared for the International Association of Law Schools Conference on Labour Law and Labour Market in the New World Economy, Milan, 20-22 May 2010.

FUNKHOUSER, E. (1992), "Migration from Nicaragua: Some Recent Evidence", *World Development*, Vol. 20, No. 8, pp. 1209-1218.

FUNKHOUSER, E. (1995), "Remittances from International Migration: A Comparison of El Salvador and Nicaragua", *The Review of Economics and Statistics*, Vol. 77, No. 1, pp. 137-146.

GAGNON, J. (2011), "Stay With Us? The Impact of Emigration on Wages in Honduras", *Working Paper* No. 300, OECD Development Centre, Paris.

GFMD (2010), Background Paper, Roundtable 2 Human mobility and human development, Session 2.2: Migration, Gender and Family, www.gfmd.org/en/gfmd-documents-library/doc_download/537--rt-22-migration-gender-and-family-english.html

GLINSKAYA, E. and M. LOKSHIN (2009), "The Effect of Male Migration on Employment Patterns of Women in Nepal", *World Bank Economic Review*, Vol. 23, No. 3, Oxford University Press, pp.481-507, November.

GÖRLICH, D., T.O. MAHMOUD and C. TREBESCH (2007), "Explaining Labour Market Inactivity in Migrant-Sending Families: Housework, Hammock or Higher Education?", *Kiel Working Paper* No. 1391.

GUBERT, F. (2002), "Do Migrants Insure those who Stay behind? Evidence from the Kayes area (Western Mali)", *Oxford Development Studies*, Vol.30, No. 3, pp.267-287.

HANSON, G. (2007a), "Emigration, Remittances and Labor Force Participation in Mexico", *INTAL-ITD Working Paper* No. 28, Washington, DC.

HANSON, G. (2007b), "Emigration, Labor Supply, and Earnings in Mexico", NBER chapters in *Mexican Immigration to the United States*, National Bureau of Economic Research Inc., Cambridge, MA, pp.289-328.

HATTON, T. and J. WILLIAMSON (2005), *Global Migration and the World Economy: Two Centuries of Policy and Performance*, MIT Press, Cambridge, MA.

ISACC (Instituto Sindical Para América Central y El Caribe) (2009), "Estudio sobre el mercado laboral y su relación con la pobreza en Honduras, Guatemala y Nicaragua", ISACC, Managua, Nicaragua.

ITZIGSOHN, J. (1995), "Migrant Remittances, Labor Markets, and Household Strategies: A Comparative Analysis of Low-Income Household Strategies in the Caribbean Basin", *Social Forces*, Vol. 74, No. 2, pp. 633-657.

JADOTTE, E. (2009), "International Migration, Remittances and Labour Supply: The Case of the Republic of Haiti", *UN-Wider Research Paper* No. 2009/28.

JAMPAKLAY, A. (2006), "Parental Absence and Children's School Enrolment: Evidence from a Longitudinal Study in Kanchanaburi, Thailand", *Asian Population Studies*, Vol. 2, No.1, pp. 93-110.

KIM, N. (2007), "The Impact of Remittances on Labor Supply: The Case of Jamaica", *Policy Research Working Paper Series* No. 4120, World Bank, Washington, DC.

LAMBERT, S., B. de la BRIERE, E. SADOULET and A. de JANVRY (2002), "The Roles of Destination, Gender and Household Composition in Explaining Remittances: An Analysis for the Dominican Sierra", *Journal of Development Economics*, Vol. 68, No. 2, pp. 309-328.

LUCAS, R.E.B. (1987), "Emigration to South Africa's Mines", *American Economic Review*, Vol. 77, No. 3, pp. 313-30.

MACHARIA, K. (2003), "Migration in Kenya and its Impact on the Labor Market", Paper prepared for Conference on African Migration in Comparative Perspective, Johannesburg, South Africa, June 4-7.

MASSEY, D. S. and E. A. PARRADO (1998), "International Migration and Business Formation in Mexico", *Social Science Quarterly*, Vol. 79, No. 1, pp. 1-20.

MISHRA, P. (2007), "Emigration and Wages in Source Countries: Evidence from Mexico", *Journal of Development Economics*, No. 82, pp.180-199.

MOHAPATRA, S., D. RATHA and A. SILWAL (2011), "Migration and Development Brief", No. 16, World Bank, Washington, DC, May.

MORA, J. J. (2010), "Remittances and Labor Participation in Colombia", Department of Economics at Universidad Icesi, mimeo.

NARAZANI, E. (2009), "Labour Supply, Remittances and the New Flat Tax in Albania", GDN-WIIW project, mimeo.

OECD (2007), *Policy Coherence for Development: Migration and Developing Countries*, OECD, Paris.

Oishi, N. (2005), "Women in Motion: Globalisation, State Policies, and Labor Migration in Asia", Stanford University Press.

Ratha, D., S. Mohapatr and E. Scheja (2011), "Impact of Migration on Economic and Social Development", *World Bank Policy Research Paper*, No. 5558, World Bank, Washington, DC.

Rodriguez, E. R. and E.R. Tiongson (2001), "Temporary Migration Overseas and Household Labor Supply: Evidence from Urban Philippines", *International Migration Review*, Vol. 35, No. 3, pp.709-725.

Silasi, G. and O.L. Simina (2007), "Romania, a Country in Need of Workers? The Bitter Taste of Strawberry Jam", *MPRA Paper* No. 14855, University Library of Munich, Germany.

Stark, O. (1991), "The Migration of Labor", Blackwell Publishing, Oxford, pp.406.

Taylor, J. E. and F. Wouterse (2008), "Migration and Income Diversification:: Evidence from Burkina Faso", *World Development*, Elsevier, Vol. 36, No. 4, pp. 625-640, April.

Thaut, L. (2009), "EU Integration & Emigration Consequences: The Case of Lithuania", *International Migration*, Vol. 47, No. 1, pp.191-233.

Tsiko (2009), "Impact of Migration on Food Security in Chiredzi, Zimbabwe", *Volens Africa*, www.volensafrica.org/Impact-of-Migration-on-Food,html?lang=en

UN (United Nations) (2011), "World Population Prospects: The 2010 Revision", CD-ROM Edition, Department of Economic and Social Affairs, Population Division, UN.

Vreyer De, P., F. Gubert and A.S. Robilliard (2010), "Are There Returns to Migration Experience? An Empirical Analysis using Data on Return Migrants and Non-Migrants in West Africa", mimeo.

Williamson, J.G. (1996), "Globalization, Convergence, and History", *The Journal of Economic History*, Cambridge University Press, Vol.56, No. 02, pp.277-306, June.

Woodruff, C. and R. Zenteno (2007), "Migration Networks and Microenterprises in Mexico", *Journal of Development Economics*, Vol. 82, pp.509-528.

Wouterse, F.S. (2008), "Migration and Technical Efficiency in Cereal Production: Evidence from Burkina Faso", *IFPRI discussion papers* No. 815, International Food Policy Research Institute (IFPRI), Washington, DC.

Wouterse, F. (2011), "Continental vs. Intercontinental Migration: An Empirical Analysis of the Impacts of Immigration Reforms on Burkina Faso", *Working Paper* No. 299, OECD Development Centre, Paris.

Yang, D. (2008), "International Migration, Remittances and Household Investment: Evidence from Philippine Migrants' Exchange Rate Shock", *The Economic Journal*, Vol. 118, No. 528, pp.591-630.

Chapter 5

Rethinking the governance of international migration

Abstract

Governments need to consider governance of migration bearing in mind the three objectives of greater flexibility of flows, improved integration and a better effect of labour mobility on development. Steps towards greater flexibility imply that host countries recognise needs, explain the benefits of immigration and foster circularity, whereby migrants may come and go more freely. Losers of immigration need to be compensated, though it may be hard to identify them. There are several ways of doing this. Better integration in the South includes the protection of migrants' rights and positive measures against discrimination as well as steps to improve social cohesion. Labour markets need to be consolidated and efforts made to put human capital to use in source countries. Migrants should be helped to get the best financial terms for their remittances. The three objectives are mutually interactive.

The book has so far highlighted three important policy challenges of international migration: the regulation of flows at the global level, the integration of immigrants, in particular in the South, and the link between migration, labour markets and development (see Figure 0.1). These challenges are closely related. Inefficient regulation, for instance, can lead to problems of integration and reduce the development potential of emigration. In the same way, the contribution of immigrants to the welfare of their communities of origin tends to be inversely proportional to their level of integration in their host societies.

Despite these interactions, few countries address all three challenges together. As shown in Chapter 2, migration policies have become increasingly restrictive, although the externalities of such policies on migrant-sending areas are rarely taken into account. Policy makers in immigrant-receiving countries generally leave discussions on the positive effects of emigration in developing countries out of the political debate, which is instead typically dominated by domestic affairs.

Yet, beyond the fact that barriers are never a sure thing, the lack of co-operation on migration issues implies an opportunity cost for the countries that implement them. The lack of reciprocity regarding the benefits derived between low and high-income countries may be illusory, since immigration constitutes a potential response to problems of labour shortage and ageing populations faced by most OECD countries (OECD, 2010).

Failing to manage immigration flows efficiently also has repercussions on social cohesion (OECD, 2011a). Local populations may feel more threatened by immigration as the number of undocumented immigrants increases. In this respect, Chapter 3, which focuses on South-South migration, draws attention to the economic and social costs of neglecting integration. It shows in particular that problems of integration in developing countries differ from those in developed countries and that specific measures are therefore required to overcome the integration challenge of migration.

Problems of regulation and integration eventually influence development in countries of emigration. As underlined in Chapter 4, the net impact of labour mobility on the welfare of migrant households depends on the trade-off between labour lost to emigration and increasing income from remittances, both of which are affected by host country immigration policies. These also have an impact on the magnitude of the effect of emigration on raising wages in developing countries. Thus, the development challenge requires minimising the negative and maximising the positive effects associated with labour mobility. It concerns not only migrant-sending but also migrant-receiving countries, in both the South and in the North.

This chapter argues that policy makers need to rethink the governance of international migration and adopt an agenda oriented towards three main objectives:

- A more flexible regulation of international migration flows;
- A better integration of immigrants;
- A greater impact of labour mobility on development.

Because these three objectives are complementary, a comprehensive governance framework should tackle all of them.

A more flexible regulation of international migration flows

The current trend towards restrictive migration policies is counter-productive. First, because controlling borders is costly both in financial and human terms. Second, because stricter border controls end up by creating more irregular immigration. And third, because many industrialised countries actually need more foreign labour, at all skill levels.

The regulation of international flows should therefore be more flexible, and not the reverse. Indeed, "as with other forms of liberalisation, greater labour mobility offers potentially significant global economic benefits" (OECD, 2004).[1] But, while a full liberalisation process may not be conceivable in the current political context, a partial liberalisation of flows, through bilateral and regional agreements (see Chapter 6), is possible.

This section argues that a road map to more flexibility should include at least three steps (Figure 5.1): acknowledging needs, fostering circularity and compensating losers.

Figure 5.1. **A road map to a more flexible regulation of flows**

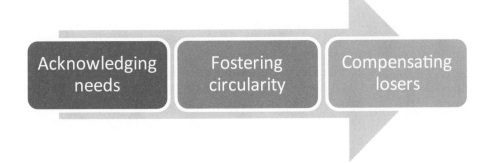

Acknowledging needs

A first step to a more flexible regulation of migration flows is for policy makers to acknowledge that their economies need immigration. As underlined in Chapter 1, the demand for foreign labour may increase as the demographic imbalance in OECD countries widens. Even though the global economic crisis contributed to significantly reducing migration flows in 2009 (OECD, 2011b), demand is likely to increase during the recovery, mainly in sectors that traditionally suffer from labour shortages, such as agriculture, catering and construction.

In many OECD countries, labour demand exceeds the supply in a growing number of sectors, thus leading to temporary or permanent shortages. Besides problems of sectoral human capital allocation, labour shortages are partly due to the ageing of the population, which implies a fall in the share of the economically active in the total population, but also an increasing demand in the care sector. Figure 5.2 illustrates the ageing population trend in OECD countries.

Figure 5.2. **Population structure by age groups in OECD countries**

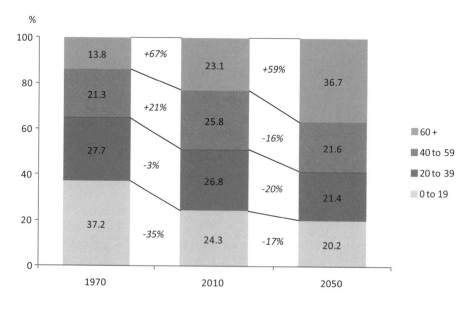

Notes: Figures with % show the change in each age group.
Source: Authors' calculations based on United Nations, World Population Prospects - 2010 Revision.

More importantly, the aggregate demand for workers is bound to rise as population ageing begins to deeply affect labour markets and social protection systems. The arrival of relatively younger workers contributes both to the renewal of the economically active population and to the financing of social protection and pension systems (Chojnicki and Ragot, 2011). In such a context, OECD countries will not only need high-skilled but also low-skilled immigrants.

Although part of the demand may be satisfied through temporary labour movements, economies require long-term immigrants too, particularly in the sectors where disequilibria may become structural, such as the health and care sectors. In this respect, the growing competition for talent not only concerns OECD countries but also emerging economies, especially in fast-growing Asia (OECD, 2011a and 2011b).

Despite the growing demand, most political leaders assume a defensive position on migration issues. Their role should rather be to communicate, through awareness campaigns for instance, the positive contribution of immigration to the economy and society. Indeed, "the planned reforms of migration policies need to involve a radical effort to enhance public knowledge and understanding of migration" rather than trying to "exploit this issue for political ends" (OECD, 2010).

Acknowledging needs does not mean overshadowing the potential costs of immigration. Low-skilled workers may feel particularly affected by the competition in the labour market generated by immigration, and problems of integration can easily spread throughout society if not tackled in time. But this is precisely why governments in host societies need to rethink their strategies, starting with fostering migration circularity.

Fostering circularity

By providing flexible labour that adjusts to the economic needs of receiving countries, circular migration represents another important step to a more flexible regulation of flows. Circular migration includes both short and long-term tenure in the host country. The difference with traditional temporary schemes, such as the US Bracero programme,[2] is that migrants have the opportunity to cross the border more than once, either in a seasonal – less than one year – or temporary – more than one year – scheme (OECD, 2007a). Not only is the level of acceptance by the locally born higher than with permanent migration, but circular migration also takes the interests of migrants, as well as the development of the origin country, better into account.

A classical example of the use of short-term circular migration is found in the agricultural sector. Instead of bringing in different workers every year, circular migration programmes offer the guarantee of return the following year. The temptation to stay on irregularly in the host country is therefore lower than with traditional temporary migration programmes (Weil, 2010). In addition, migrants can save money without breaking the link with their families for extended periods, and the contribution to the development in the community of origin is stronger.

In the long term, return can also foster circularity and increase tolerance of immigration. When local populations know that immigrants will eventually return to their countries of origin, opposition to immigration decreases. Return can also help leverage development in origin countries, thanks to financial and human capital acquired in the host country. In this respect, several European countries have assistance programmes aimed at getting immigrants to accept voluntary return to their countries.

But return also needs to be circular. Indeed, on many occasions the reason why migrants do not return to their country of origin is because they are not assured of re-entry into the host country. In fact, one of the main factors why family reunification significantly increased in Europe after 1975 is related to the closing of borders to economic immigrants. Those that knew they could no longer circulate freely preferred to bring their families to the host country rather than return home.

Even though circular migration brings benefits, it represents a way for receiving countries to avoid the integration costs related to immigration, such as public expenditure on education, health and housing (Akers Chacón and Davis, 2006). It is cheaper, both economically and socially, to bring in temporary labour rather than allow foreign workers to settle permanently. Nevertheless, such policy comes at a cost, as employers must retrain new workers. Keeping previously trained immigrants would, in effect, be more efficient (OECD, 2008).

For this reason permanent migration must also be considered. As underlined previously, industrialised economies require long-term migration and many migrants would prefer to stay and settle in the host country. This implies acknowledging that there are losers in the process and that they must be compensated.

Compensating losers

A third step to a more flexible regulation of migration flows is the implementation of compensation mechanisms. The net positive effect of migration does not mean that everyone benefits from a more liberalised process. Just as when trade is opened up, workers, typically those with lower skills and little experience, face greater competition in the labour market with more immigration (OECD, 2004). But compensating losers is more difficult for immigration than it is for trade and capital (Felbermay and Kohler, 2007).

Beyond reasons of equity and fairness, compensating losers is essential to facilitate political support for policies aiming at fully benefiting from globalisation. But it is difficult to find a Pareto efficient equilibrium: a change in policy that makes at least one person better off and no one worse off. One possible way is through a redistribution of the gains derived from migration, for instance by subsidising directly the work of the lowest-skilled (Sinn, 2005).

The difficulty lies in defining the winners and losers. If by winners and losers, we mean having a migrant status *vs.* being locally born, the division can easily be made. But, if policy makers aim at compensating losers based on skill level, the distinction is blurry. Instead of skills, compensation should be based on income (Saß, 2010), as income can act as a proxy for skill level.

Several types of compensation have been discussed, but contain flaws in their efficiency in redistributing the benefits or in their implementation. Countries of origin benefit from welfare-improving effects such as remittances, skill-enhancing return migration, entrepreneurship and technology spillovers. There has been discussion on asking major immigrant source countries to offer concessions. These concessions can take the shape of more favourable trade relationships, such as less stringent quotas.

The problem is that this approach does not directly compensate the losers. Instead, the economy gets boosted in two ways: businesses import much needed labour and then enjoy trade concessions with other countries. While the overall gain may be large, it may be viewed as favouring the rich and neglecting those really losing from migration. This approach also discriminates against very poor countries and people, in effect eliminating them from the market and reducing their chances of reducing poverty through migration.

Another instrument proposed is instead allowing immigrants fully to enjoy the economic benefits of their labour but limiting their access to the welfare state, at least for a certain period of time. Immigrants with long-term tenure could then see access granted, as long as they pay taxes. Access could be given after a certain number of years, or gradually from year 1, according to the principle of selectively delayed integration (Richter, 2004). The downside here relates to human rights and minimum welfare. Disconnecting workers from the right to subsidised healthcare, day care, housing and child education can increase inequality and damage social cohesion. In addition, removing a significant amount of benefits may turn away too many immigrants willing to work in the country – a direct loss of needed labour.

Immigration countries can also anticipate problems and deal with them head-on: that is, by ensuring that competition in the labour market is not an issue beforehand, through an efficient balance of high and low-skilled migrants. One possible way is to improve bilateral matching systems between home and host country. Through a visa auction system, for instance, host countries can increase the selection process of immigration by ensuring that only those qualified, even low-skilled workers, enter the country at the right price – the proceeds being used to alleviate tax burdens or train those without work (Freeman, 2006; Richter, 2004).

The most logical instrument is probably a system of tax-based compensation (Hatton and Williamson, 2005). All other things being equal, immigrants would pay higher tax rates than native workers. The revenue collected would then compensate those affected by immigration. Not only is this ideal in terms of limiting the negative pressures of immigration, but the proceeds could also be used to alleviate the tax burden on native-born workers. Since a rising number of immigrants implies more public health and education expenditure (Boeri, 2010),[3] the locally born might indeed feel concerned by the fiscal costs associated with higher immigration rates in welfare states. Another option is to tax instead employers (Hatton and Williamson, 2005).

In the end, the aim remains the same: to tax the benefits of immigration from those benefiting and use the proceeds to help those who lose or come under stress. Side payments have thus the potential to be Pareto efficient: immigrants still earn more than they would have in their home country, employers can still access much-needed labour (to a certain point) and local workers pay less tax. This can then be combined with incentives for immigrants to move to cities and regions within the country where labour is in most need.

The proceeds can go to training programmes to enhance the human capital of workers losing their jobs. This would imply efficiently pinpointing the sectors most affected and the type of workers and training needed in the market. An example of this mechanism is the extension of the US Trade Adjustment Assistance Program to those losing their jobs because of immigration (Trachtman, 2009).[4]

A better integration of immigrants

Migrant stocks are higher between countries in the South than between South and North. Many developing countries have answered the challenge by increasing the management of their borders, with little thought given to managing immigrants inside their country. But how can integration be managed in the South? Even in the relatively richer North, the very nature of integration programmes is a major source of political debate.

As shown in Chapter 3, the social and economic situation in the South presents challenges different from those more typical in the North. Therefore, the integration debate in the South is likely not to be the same as in the North. In particular, an integration policy requires a strategy that incorporates the particularities and field realities of developing economies, such as the high circularity of migration, prevalent informal labour market activities and low relative deprivation between the locally born and immigrants.

Policy making cannot accordingly solely focus on immigrants, primarily because the locally born are also deprived of many basic advantages and rights. For many reasons, including *jus sanguinis* laws, internal politics, isolated groups and illiteracy, the locally born may be part of a phenomenon called "blurred citizenship" (Sadiq, 2009), which means they are born in, and part of, the nation, but not necessarily included in its citizenry. How can policy makers reach out to immigrants when some of their locally born citizens are even more disempowered? Much deeper and generalised policies are perhaps more imperative. To avoid immigrants from being marginalised in the general reform process, however, specific measures to protect and include them should be taken, particularly for the most vulnerable. But implementing such policies implies administrative and financial constraints.

In many cases, decision makers simply do not know how to approach the situation. Immigrant integration is still a hotly debated issue in most countries and a clear-cut solution does not exist. The *status quo* is a likely strategy for governments that claim a "liberal approach" to immigrant integration. In addition, even though many countries are benefiting from the boost in commodity prices over the last two decades (OECD, 2011a), most countries in the South still do not have the adequate resources fully to deal with the expensive measures of migration regulation (Chapter 2) and immigrant integration taken in the North.[5]

But despite limited financial and administrative capacity, many developing countries are currently dealing with integration. A better integration of immigrants is indeed possible. Priority should be given especially to the protection of rights, the fight against discrimination and incorporation into society (Figure 5.3).

Figure 5.3. **The priorities of integration policies**

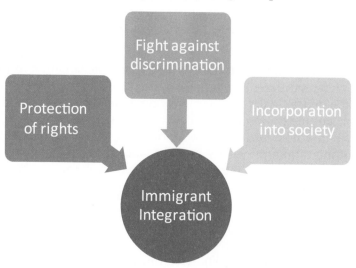

Protecting rights

Perhaps the biggest hurdle to immigrant integration in the South is the prevalent violation of human and civil rights. The lack of rights particularly hits both short and long-term workers, while transit migrants are a particular category of migrants with few rights. Normative and institutional structures combating the vulnerable nature of certain migrants are on the rise,[6] but enforcement remains low. The following guidelines would help guide immigrants away from a violation of their rights.

First is the extension of civil rights and protection for all members of society, regardless of status. This implies the inclusion of all members of society, including irregular immigrants, in all economic and social reforms. It also implies governmental support and promotion of the right for immigrants to organise, assemble and represent themselves or the groups of which they are part, including the freedom to practise and share elements of culture, but also to participate in the culture of the host country. In Argentina, for instance, the 2003 Migration Law gives migrants free legal representation, the right to a fair trial before expulsion and the right to family reunification (Jachimowicz, 2006). In Costa Rica the importance of human rights in school curriculum guidelines has also gradually increased over time (Shiman, 2009).

Second is to ensure that employers of immigrants guarantee their registration and minimum accommodation. Many employers exploit the fact that immigrants represent cheaper labour and are without rights or adequate legal representation. Insisting that they register employees implies that migrants can access basic public services. In early 2011 for instance, Bangladesh (through the Bangladesh Association for International Recruitment Agencies) and Saudi Arabia (through the Saudi National Recruitment Committee) struck an agreement on migration recruitment by pre-establishing four categories of workers, their salaries and age limits and appointed a human rights association to which migrants can voice their complaints in cases of violation. According to both parties, recruitment will surpass 10 000 workers per month.

Third is to target the perpetrators of violations. This can be done by launching awareness-raising campaigns for the local population, immigration officials, police officers and local leaders. More aggressively, tougher sanctions can also be imposed on wrongdoers. In this respect, Mexico has adopted a series of measures to protect transit migrants, for instance by establishing refuges for children, financing campaigns on the rights of migrants and prosecuting the perpetrators of human rights violations, in particular police officers.

Donors also have a role to play in curbing human rights violations through public interventions. In 2010, for instance, the UNESCO Steering Committee of the West Africa Institute (WAI) created a research institute on regional immigrant integration in West Africa. The general objective of the WAI is to advance knowledge on West African regional integration and to provide decision makers with related policy options conducive to development, peace and the protection of human rights in the sub-region. In addition, the International Organization for Migration (IOM) held two sub-national workshops followed by a series of local consultations on "the protection of vulnerable persons on the move" in eight member countries of the Economic Community of West African States (ECOWAS).[7]

Fighting against discrimination

All workers, including immigrants, should be free from all forms of discrimination in the labour market. Even in contexts of strong legislation against xenophobia and discrimination, the largely informal labour market ensures that unfavourable practices remain. A relatively high number of immigrants are stuck in bad and/or informal jobs compared to locals, with little in terms of social security; many are pushed further into unsafe and hazardous jobs. The barriers that segregate the labour market make it easy to discriminate against immigrants in terms of pay, housing, land rights and education. Stereotypes clearly play a big role, but targeted policy can curb the outcome.

A first step is to deal with discrimination directly. The dismantling of discriminatory laws has been gradual, but many practices remain, notably in the field of religion. Policy makers can target local perceptions of immigrants and tone down myths by launching awareness campaigns, and helping ensure multi-ethnic and unbiased journalism.

A second step is to deal with informality. This can be done with adapted social security measures (basic housing and health) which take into account vulnerable workers and dangerous jobs. Labour market reforms must ensure that they cover all workers, and not only those with formal jobs. One way to do this is by regularising immigrants and making it easier for them to circulate legally between home and host country. This gives the benefit to the host country of knowing the number and characteristics of immigrants in their country, while paving the way for many of them to access jobs and services such as health and housing.

While regularisation and naturalisation are usually uncommon in the South, some countries have recently taken this route, including Argentina, Barbados, Costa Rica, Malaysia,[8] South Africa and Thailand.[9] During 2009 and 2010, Costa Rica, for instance, passed a series of regulations which eventually evolved into the General Law on Migration and Alien Status. Immigrants now benefit from greater protection and can leave the country for up to two years without losing the right to work in Costa Rica. The problem with these programmes is primarily related to the cost of registration, which can amount to several times the monthly wage immigrants earn. Moreover, the process (or the renewal) can be complicated. Since many immigrants in the South are illiterate, regularisation may be out of reach for many of them.

Another problem is that many immigrants do not have the proper paperwork to apply for regularisation, either because of corruption in the home country, bilateral conflicts, *jus sanguinis* laws or because they were part of the blurred citizenry in their home country and never obtained formal identification papers. Moreover, the widespread circulation of fraudulent papers does not help the process. Many immigrants are indeed rendered stateless through immigration. Countries often use the good will generated from regularising irregular migrants to restrict migration and step up enforcement.

Thailand was criticised in years past for placing too much emphasis on attracting skilled migrants with the reform of the Board of Investment (BOI) in 2001 and the implementation of the "elitecard", granting special access to skilled workers to many benefits in the country (UN-Habitat, 2010), and pushing aside the integration of lower-skilled migrants. But in 2003 Thailand granted all immigrants access to the national health care system and, in collaboration with the IOM, launched a migrant health programme focused on the border with Myanmar. The objective was to improve migrant health and well-being, regardless of immigration status. In accordance with the health interventions, the programme now also officially regularises migrants, by providing them with a one-year visa to work in the country after a full medical check.

Argentina also opened the right to health and educational services to all migrants in 2003, regardless of their status (Jachimowicz, 2006). Through the National Registry of Rural Workers and Employers (RENATRE) programme, unemployment schemes were also extended to agricultural workers, regardless of their immigration status. Employers contribute 1.5% of their worker's monthly salary to the scheme.[10] In conjunction with these changes, the country has also paved the way for legal status through a programme called "Patria Grande".

Finally, policy makers can help ease bureaucratic processes with respect to immigration, thus ensuring segregation from the locally born cannot take place, at least formally and legally. This includes the removal of bureaucratic rules for employers wishing to hire qualified immigrants, but also making institutions more flexible by, for instance, allowing immigrants to own or rent real estate, invest, and pay the same school fees as locals.

Incorporating immigrants into society

Immigrants are often pushed to the bottom of their host country's class system, usually because of their low levels of material wealth and (perceived) human capital. For those staying long term, a better incorporation requires better jobs, more skills, access to services and less segregation. Most long-term policies for their incorporation include those dealing with basic rights and fighting discrimination noted earlier. They also generally apply to all workers in the economy, not only immigrants; this is especially true with respect to public services for informal workers. But a few key objectives can specifically help their incorporation, without taking anything away from locals.

The first is to facilitate job-matching between host and home country. This ensures that immigrants are not deceived by rumours and word-of-mouth demand, but are drawn by actual job offers. This can be quite effective for seasonal work, particularly when home and host country institutions work efficiently together.

In the second place, and for those staying for the longer term, access to education for immigrant children can hasten integration and understanding, through spillovers of language and culture. For adults specific hands-on and vocational training for jobs in high demand in the country can boost the matching mechanism.

The third element is a facilitation of housing arrangements and avoidance of the creation of ghettos by immigrants crowding together. Ensuring that formal restrictions for immigrants to access housing are lowered partially ensures that they do not end up in ghettos.

However, the policies above constitute pieces in a larger puzzle. Box 5.1 provides an example of how South Africa turned a potentially disastrous situation into a net gain for the country by taking a comprehensive approach to immigrant integration.

Box 5.1. **Migration policy and social cohesion in South Africa**

In May 2008, a series of riots against immigrants from nearby countries in a township of Johannesburg spread to the cities of Gauteng, Western Cape, Cape Town, Durban and other provinces. By the end, 62 immigrants had been killed, several hundred injured, thousands displaced and many properties looted and destroyed. The wave of violence occurred at a time of rising immigration (especially from Zimbabwe) and a general deterioration of socio-economic conditions in the most deprived areas of South Africa.

The government immediately condemned the xenophobic attacks and deployed police to restore order and arrest suspects. It also created temporary camps and implemented re-integration plans. Following the wave of violence, social cohesion and integration policies became a matter of concern for the government and a central subject of study, and in August 2008 the "Migration and Social Cohesion" Project was launched by the Institute for Democracy in South Africa (IDASA), an independent public interest organisation. It aims to fight the negative perception of migration as a threat to social cohesion and to communicate the ways in which migrants can be positively incorporated into society. It follows two principal assumptions: that integration enhances the contribution of migrants to the economic, social, cultural and political development of the host society, and that diversity is an opportunity and a source of enrichment.

To foster the participation of migrants in South African society, the project promotes research and publication. After gathering policy-relevant information, the team organises workshops for policy makers, so that they can implement proactive programmes and change the legal framework. The project also encourages collaborative engagement and mutually reinforcing relationships between migrants and locals. Finally, it improves public awareness of the role, status and contribution of immigrants.

One significant lesson derived from the experience of the project has been the importance of beginning at the local level, where the process of integration occurs primarily. City projects have thus been implemented in Cape Town, with the establishment of a loan and savings scheme, and in Johannesburg, through a migrants' help desk. Such initiatives ease integration by encouraging interaction between immigrants and citizens. A second way to enhance social cohesion is through partnerships between the government and other stakeholders and the involvement of a large range of actors at all levels. The IDASA project also argues for legislation as the preferred tool to guarantee equality and non-discrimination and to fight against exploitation and abuse of migrants (in particular women, children and undocumented migrants).

A greater impact of labour mobility on development

The formulation of policies linking migration and development is based on the idea that it is possible to enhance welfare in migrant-sending countries through the efficient management of international movements. Over the last two decades sending countries have accordingly tried to place migration into the mainstream of their development strategies, by focusing policies on the accumulation and repatriation of three kinds of capital:

- **Financial capital**, through policies aimed at lowering the costs of sending remittances, and channelling them towards productive investment;

- **Human capital**, through policies intended to promote the temporary and permanent return of high-skilled migrants, and the participation of scientific diasporas in transnational networks or research projects;

- **Social capital**, through co-operation with hometown associations (HTAs) to attract collective remittances, used to finance local initiatives, particularly infrastructure and educational projects.

In parallel, a number of OECD countries, such as France, the Netherlands, Spain and Sweden, have included migration in their international co-operation strategies (see Chapter 2). Most of these policies aim at:

- **Fostering productive investment**, by increasing the financial capacity of future investors and strengthening their entrepreneurial skills;

- **Promoting temporary and circular migration**, with the idea of providing flexible labour that adjusts to industrialised economies' needs, but also of maximising the contribution of migrants to the development of the community of origin;

- **Encouraging return**, not only through financial aid but also technical assistance and training programmes.

Previous publications from the OECD Development Centre (in particular, OECD 2007a and 2007b) analysed policies linking migration and development in detail, highlighting the benefits but also the potential shortcomings. In this book, we focus on one specific aspect of the migration-development nexus, namely the impact of emigration on labour markets.

As described in Chapter 4, the emigration of part of the labour force impacts the home country's labour market in two principal ways. First, the departure of a productive household member has a net negative impact due to the direct loss of labour. Second, remittances have a net positive effect, by increasing household income. In many developing countries, these effects are amplified by the fact that the population is essentially rural and that migration is primarily regional. The lost-labour effect is thus considerable while the remittance effect remains limited.

The main objective of public policy should therefore be to optimise the impact of labour mobility on development, effectively minimising the negative impact from lost labour and the positive impact from remittances. To this end, this section is centred on four main priorities (Figure 5.4): *i)* the consolidation of labour markets; *ii)* the accumulation of human capital; *iii)* the promotion of financial democracy; and *iv)* the strengthening of social cohesion.

Figure 5.4. **Labour mobility and development: priorities**

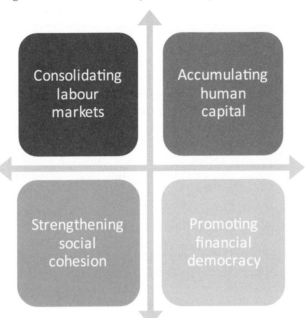

Consolidating labour markets

In reducing the negative effect of the lost-labour effect, the first priority is the consolidation of labour markets. In this respect migrant-sending countries play an important role. They can, in particular, put in place policies that aim to reduce the negative impact associated with South-South flows (where generally the negative lost-labour effect dominates the positive remittance effect) while leveraging the positive impact of South-North flows (since the positive remittance effect dominates the negative lost-labour effect). Policy makers are nevertheless constrained since migration policies, especially those that concern migration to OECD countries, are out of their control.

The negative aspect of lost labour is essentially due to the absence of a working labour market, as households cannot adequately compensate for the departure of productive members. It is therefore important that sending countries adopt measures integrating labour markets, locally and nationally. This implies, in particular, a gradual move towards more formal economic activity. The creation of national job centres, for instance, is an effective way of consolidating labour markets while also contributing to the reduction of the lost-labour effect.

Migrant-receiving countries are also well positioned to implement migration policies that leverage the positive impact of labour mobility for development. As explained previously, adding flexibility in migration schemes would reinforce the link between migration and development with the added benefit of not affecting the objectives of migration control. In this respect circular programmes help countries benefit from migration by minimising the lost-labour effect, particularly in the agricultural sector. For the home country, circular migration preserves the continuity of agricultural activities throughout the year, especially when agricultural cycles in the home and receiving countries happen at different times of the year. The opportunity to return each season constitutes an additional factor of income stability for migrants; the steady source of income allows them to invest in their home country.

Accumulating human capital

The second priority is the accumulation of human capital, which can offset the negative lost-labour effect through an increase in specific skills. Instead of fighting brain drain, which in most circumstances has proved to be difficult and ineffective, policies should turn towards brain circulation (Johnson and Regets, 1998). To maximise the contribution of high-skilled migrants to the development of the home country, policy makers can promote the temporary or permanent return of high-skilled migrants as well as the participation of scientific diasporas in transnational networks or research projects.

Permanent return is a delicate issue, above all for high-skilled workers, who may experience difficulty finding employment opportunities matching their skills and interests. However, developing countries can encourage returns by giving loans instead of grants to students willing to study abroad (OECD, 2007a). In cases where students benefit from a grant and thereafter stay permanently in the host country,[11] the state loses its investment; with a loan, students have to pay the money back and the state is guaranteed not to lose. However if students decide to return home, the state can forgive loan repayments, turning the *ex ante* loan into an *ex post* grant.

Some countries have succeeded in attracting back talent by creating favourable conditions for returnees, for instance by recognising foreign diplomas and offering a wage premium to high-skilled returnees, particularly for public service. China, for example, adopted in the 1990s a series of preferential measures for returnees, such as elevating their professional titles, allowing them to work in cities other than those from which they had emigrated and increasing support for higher education and scientific research (Zweig, 2006).

But, for most countries, it is easier to promote brain circulation by encouraging high-skilled workers to return for short-term visits and to teach or take part in co-operative projects. This generates positive externalities through transfers of technology and information.

Human capital strategies also rely on the capacity of public authorities to consolidate scientific diasporas and mobilise both human and financial resources (Kuznetsov and Sabel, 2006). High-skilled expatriates can co-operate on research projects of interest for the development of their countries of origin. The rapid improvements in telecommunications have enabled the expansion of transnational networks, strengthening the links with members of the scientific community abroad (Meyer, 2010). Expatriate talent can also help transfer technology and knowledge, even when the conditions at home are not necessarily optimal. Despite the lack of a real innovation policy in India, the diaspora invested in the software industry, thus creating the basis for high-tech development (Devane, 2006).

It is also possible to link productive return and transfers of knowledge and technology through a training policy oriented towards immigrants and based on the technological needs of developing countries. Trained immigrants can go back to their countries and work in firms that benefit from technology transfers, for instance in the information technology and solar energy sectors. In Sweden the Solar Energy Foundation supports a project called Solartech that provides training on solar energy to African immigrants who have the opportunity to go back to their home countries and work in firms that benefit from the transfer of technology provided by the foundation's programme.[12] These types of initiatives foster not only the reintegration of returnees but also local development.

Finally, a push for regional brain circulation would yield a more efficient allocation of human capital between developing countries. Such a policy could focus on the following three points:

- Student mobility: the lack of financial resources in universities in developing countries can be overcome through the creation of specialised academic clusters. Reinforced by scholarship-supported mobility, this would have the benefit of attracting students from other countries in the region.

- High-skilled workers: creating and improving conditions so that experts and qualified labour can access quality jobs in the region. These conditions should be adapted to both short and more structural, long-term demand.

- Transnational scientific networks: supporting scientific co-operation through the development of regional projects while incorporating communities in the diaspora.

Promoting financial democracy

The third priority is the promotion of financial democracy: that is, a better knowledge of, and better access to, financial services (Terry and Wilson, 2005). By leveraging the financial potential of immigrants, financial democracy helps maximise the positive effect of remittances. It implies in particular lowering the costs of sending remittances, increasing the financial capacity of potential investors, and strengthening their entrepreneurial skills.

The G8 countries agreed, during the 2009 Summit in L'Aquila in Italy, on the "5x5 Objective", which is the reduction of the global average cost of transferring remittances by five percentage points (from 10% to 5%) in five years. Several European countries have opened public websites that compare the costs of sending remittances to help immigrants find the cheapest way to send money home.[13] The underlying idea is that as long as information on the cost of sending remittances is difficult to obtain, money remitters do not have the incentive to lower transaction costs. By easing access to information, these websites promote competition between financial intermediaries, and hence a drop in the cost of sending money home and an increase in opportunities to invest in productive projects.

Strategies aimed at channelling remittances towards productive investment usually target the families that receive the money or migrants themselves, when they decide to return. Some countries such as Brazil, Ecuador and the Philippines or donors such as the *Deutsche Gesellschaft für Internationale Zusammenarbeit* (*GIZ*) in Germany, offer technical, financial and legal assistance to would-be entrepreneurs, who in general do not have the specific training to create their own businesses. The Filipino government also offers subsidies to returnees to buy productive assets.

Another interesting experience in terms of productive investment is the organisation of housing fairs by several migrant-sending countries, such as Colombia, Honduras and Mexico. Such fairs take place in the countries of immigration, (for example, the United States and Spain), and gather migrant communities, property developers and banking institutions. They contribute to stimulating the housing sector by enabling migrants to invest in their origin countries.

Financial democracy also rests on financial education (Terry and Wilson, 2005). The Global Financial Education Programme (GFEP), for instance, through its module "Remittances: Make the Most of Them", seeks to make immigrants and recipient families aware of the importance of employing formal banking services. It also provides information about the remittances market. The purpose is to ensure that people are better acquainted with the relevant legislation, entities and services, and feel more confident with the financial system. Financial literacy helps both immigrants and remittance-receivers define financial goals, select appropriate products and plan for the future (GFEP, 2007). The GFEP has conducted several education campaigns in both migration-receiving (Germany, Italy and the Netherlands among them) and remittance-receiving countries (including Ecuador, Ghana, Mexico, the Philippines and Turkey).

Strengthening social cohesion

The fourth priority of migration-based development strategies should be aimed at strengthening social cohesion, not only in the countries of destination (see Chapter 3), but also in the countries of origin. Policies linking migration and development tend indeed to focus on economic rather than social outcomes. Policy agendas give priority to the productive use of remittances and the return of talent, but tend to forget the social repercussions of emigration, particularly for those left behind (see Chapter 4).

By generating problems related to social cohesion, family disintegration not only affects migrant communities, but also entire countries (see Box 4.2). For this reason public authorities need to apply adequate and timely solutions to a problem that will be growing as the care drain phenomenon continues to gain amplitude:

- Prevention is fundamental in making migrants aware of the risks of migrating without documentation, being victim of human trafficking and leaving children behind. Information campaigns can be promoted through a variety of media but also schools, migrant organisations and community groups (*e.g.* religious communities) and NGOs.

- Support for those left behind can improve their welfare and minimise any social disruption caused by emigration. Such support may take different forms, including legal and financial assistance and general guidance, for instance through safety-net programmes to support households with absent migrants (*e.g.* Philippines and Sri Lanka) and granting scholarships for children left behind. Guidance on parenting and campaigns on how to address parenting problems, depression and mental health issues resulting from migration for those left behind are also needed.

- Support for care-givers is required to minimise the negative impact of the loss of care workers. This can be achieved by reinforcing the care arrangement for those left behind. Financial support should address the provision of child allowances directly to the care provider regardless of employment, providing more resources to schools and teachers to monitor the welfare of children and take action when necessary. Legal support is also needed through legislation on domestic work in the event that migrant-sending households employ migrant women from within the country or women from poorer backgrounds to fill the demand for care work.

- As the negative impact of parental migration depends on the length of the separation and the frequency of contacts, methods of linking families by distance must be addressed. Providing better and cheaper telecommunication tools while training migrants and their households to use them is essential. More flexible migration schemes would also facilitate and increase the number of contacts between separated household members.

But emigration not only generates social costs; it also represents an opportunity to strengthen social cohesion in sending countries. The links discussed earlier with diasporas can also generate social capital (Guarnizo, 2003).[14] In addition to brain circulation, diaspora links help attract collective remittances. These funds, raised by HTAs or channelled through Internet community networks, are used to finance local initiatives, particularly infrastructure and educational projects.

Remittance-related programmes, such as those implemented by Mexico[15] and El Salvador,[16] have the advantage of enabling migrants to contribute not only to the welfare of their own families, but also to the improvement of the economic and social conditions in their local communities. The state can take advantage of the implication of migrant associations to increase public investment projects in the areas that need it more, in particular social protection programmes. By serving as a stimulus for the government to act the effect of collective remittances can be leveraged on both social cohesion and development.

Interactions and complementarities of objectives

Each objective developed in this chapter responds to a specific policy challenge: regulation, integration and development. But each policy challenge also interacts with the others (see Figure 0.1). A comprehensive governance framework therefore needs to include all three objectives and consider their complementarities (Figure 5.5).

Figure 5.5. **The complementarity of objectives**

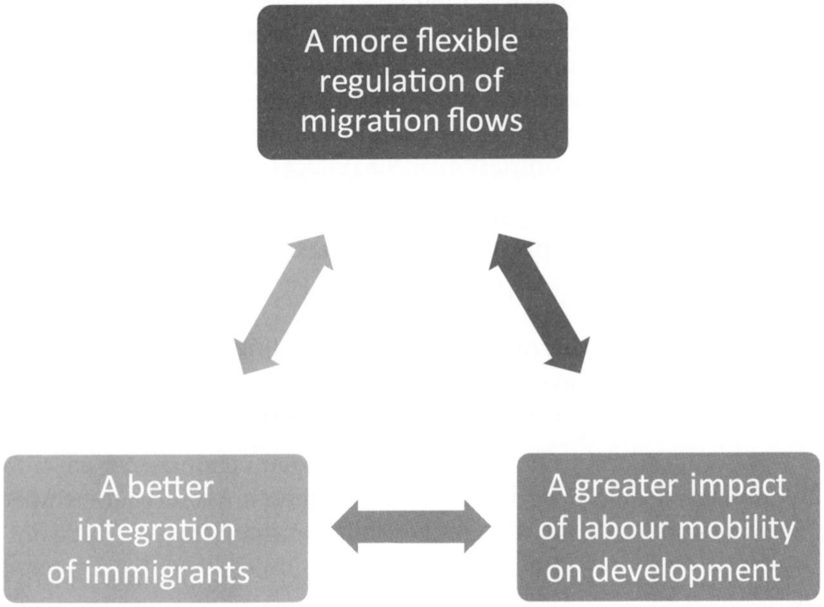

A more flexible regulation of migration means that the number of undocumented immigrants would significantly decrease, while circular migration would increase.[17] As a result, countries of immigration could better tackle the integration challenge. Fewer undocumented immigrants imply less human trafficking, labour informality and ghettoisation, which would eventually help raise the tolerance threshold in host societies. In addition, public authorities could better focus on the needs of immigrants, both temporary and permanent, while also taking into account the locally born. This is particularly important in developing countries with high levels of immigration.

Less restrictive migration policies would also contribute better to development in countries of origin. Temporary and circular migration programmes would in particular help origin countries benefit from migration by minimising the lost-labour effect, particularly in the agricultural sector. Circular migration indeed preserves the continuity of agricultural activities throughout the year, especially when agricultural cycles in the home and receiving countries happen at different times of the year. The opportunity of returning each season constitutes an additional income stability factor for migrants. The steady source of income also enables migrants to invest in their home countries.

Better integrated immigrants also have more opportunity to improve economic and social conditions in their communities of origin. In this respect, naturalisation policies constitute a good example of policies that contribute both to the integration of immigrants and to the development of the countries of origin, in particular by increasing the net positive impact of remittances. Obtaining host country nationality facilitates the integration of immigrants into the labour market for four primary reasons (OECD, 2010):

- Naturalised migrants have access to jobs from which previously they were excluded, in particular in the public sector;

- It is easier for firms to hire national rather than foreign workers;

- The fact that immigrants have a choice over naturalisation constitutes a signal to employers about the will to integrate (through language, customs), which are positive values of employability;

- Naturalisation facilitates greater investment in human capital, not only for immigrants who expect a higher return, but also for employers who see naturalisation as a guarantee of stability.

A better insertion into the labour market means immigrants benefit from not only more stable but also higher income, which they can then send home. This argument is nuanced, since a naturalised immigrant is more likely to have his family with him and as a consequence send less money back home. However, naturalised immigrants, and in a more general way well integrated immigrants, can be more inclined to send collective remittances through HTAs, and contribute to social and educational investment in their home communities. Likewise, high-skilled workers can integrate into professional or scientific diasporas and participate in local projects useful for development.

Finally, a better impact of labour mobility on development has a reverse effect. Indeed, more opportunities in home countries means return migration increases and the number of immigrants settling permanently decreases, thus facilitating both the regulation and integration processes.

To optimise complementarities between the three objectives defined in this chapter, and to maximise the benefits of migration, both for sending and receiving countries, policy makers need to revise the current governance framework. Chapter 6 argues that this is possible, by forming partnerships for better migration management and development.

Notes

1. Moses and Letnes (2004) estimate that the world efficiency gain from partial withdrawal of mobility restrictions (less than 1%) would have represented around 10% of world GDP in 1998. Hatton (2007) argues that these gains are ten times as large as the benefits from trade liberalisation.

2. By attracting mainly Mexican temporary labour, the American *Bracero programme*, which ran from 1942 and 1964, was a way for the US agricultural sector to deal with labour shortages caused by the participation of the country in World War-II (Hatton and Williamson, 2005).

3. In a certain way, irregular immigration enables receiving countries to benefit from more and cheaper labour without having to bear the fiscal burden (Hanson, 2010). However, authorised migration inflows help finance pay-as-you-go pension systems, particularly in European countries (Chojnicki *et al.*, 2005). Higher immigration and regularisation measures also increase tax revenues. The regularisation of undocumented immigrants in the United States may generate USD 4.5 billion to USD 5.4 billion in additional net tax revenue (Hinojosa-Ojeda, 2010).

4. The US Department of Labor Trade Adjustment Assistance (TAA) for Workers Program assists workers who have lost their jobs or have suffered a reduction of hours and wages as a result of increased imports or shifts in production outside US territory. The TAA Program aims to help participants obtain new jobs, ensure they retain employment and earn wages comparable to their prior employment. In its current state, it does not cover workers who become unemployed as a result of immigration.

5. The Obama administration's proposed budget for 2012 included immigrant integration programmes worth USD 20 million.

6. In 2000, a set of three protocols (the Palermo Protocols) on trafficking were adopted by the United Nations. Since its entry into force in 2003 many countries have passed strong legislation against human trafficking. In 2002 and 2003, Benin, Nigeria and Togo signed a series of agreements, together with United Nations Office on Drugs and Crime (UNODC), on common border issues, including trafficking. The signing followed earlier agreements by Côte d'Ivoire with Senegal and Mali on child labour in 2000.

7. Benin, Burkina Faso, Ghana, Liberia, Niger, Nigeria, Sierra Leone and Togo. Information available at: www.iom.int/jahia/Jahia/policy-research/regional-consultative-processes/

8. The last round of regularisation took place in July 2011, during which immigrants were provided with biometric identification cards.

9. The last round of regularisation took place in June and July 2011.

10. Annex to the Global Forum for Migration and Development Roundtable 2.1 Background Paper (WHO/IOM).

11. On average, around 21% of foreign students in OECD countries do not return to their countries of origin (OECD, 2010).

12. See www.solarenergyfoundation.com/.

13. Among them, France (www.envoidargent.fr), Italy (www.mandasoldiacasa.it) and Spain (www.remesas.org).

14. Social capital is a public good that includes ties of trust between the members of society (Coleman, 1990). It implies the respect for collective commitments, thus strengthening social cohesion. Social capital has a positive impact on other forms of capital, such as financial and human capital.

15. The Programa Iniciativa Ciudadana 3x1 was created in Mexico in 2002. For every dollar invested in local development by Mexican HTAs, the government brings three more dollars: one comes from the federal government, another from the state government and a third from the municipality. The 3x1 Programme has helped fund a wide range of initiatives including social and educational projects (Vásquez Mota, 2005).

16. The Salvadoran programme Unidos por la Solidaridad aims at co-ordinating the anti-poverty efforts of public authorities with the private sector and associations of Salvadorans living abroad. The funds provided by contributors are administered by the Social Investment Fund for Local Development, which distributes available resources through open calls for grant proposals from local communities.

17. Would-be migrants are rational agents who are not only attracted by wage differentials but also employment opportunities (Todaro, 1969). If there are limited opportunities, as in periods of economic crisis, foreign workers do not come. Moreover, many immigrants already in the host country return home, at least when they have the guarantee they can emigrate again later (Keeley, 2009). This is essentially what happened with a number of immigrants from Eastern Europe living in Ireland and the United Kingdom following the 2008 economic crisis.

References

AKERS CHACÓN, J. and M. Davis (2006), *No One Is Illegal: Fighting Racism and State Violence on the US-Mexico Border*, Haymarket Books, Chicago, IL.

BOERI, T. (2010), "Immigration to the Land of Redistribution", *Economica*, Vol. 77, No. 4, pp. 651-687.

CHOJNICKI, X., F. DOCQUIER and L. RAGOT (2005), "L'immigration choisie face aux défis économiques du vieillissement démographique", *Revue économique* Vol.56, No. 6, pp. 1359-1384.

CHOJNICKI, X. and L. RAGOT (2011), "Immigration, vieillissement démographique et financement de la protection sociale : une évaluation par l'équilibre général calculable appliqué à la France", *CEPII Working Papers, 2011-13*, CEPII, Paris.

COLEMAN, J. (1990), *Foundations of Social Theory*, Harvard University Press, Cambridge, MA.

DEVANE, R. (2006), "The Dynamics of Diaspora Networks: Lessons of Experience", in KUZNETSOV, Y. (ed.), *Diaspora Networks and the International Migration of Skills*, World Bank, Washington, DC, pp. 59-67.

FELBERMAYR, G. J. and KOHLER, W. (2007), "Immigration and Native Welfare", *International Economic Review*, Vol. 48, No. 3, pp. 731-758.

FREEMAN, R.B. (2006), "People Flows in Globalization", *Journal of Economic Perspectives*, Vol. 20, No. 2, pp. 145-170.

GFEP (2007), "Remittances: Make the Most of Them", *Research Note*, Global Financial Education Programme.

GUARNIZO, L.E. (2003), "The Economics of Transnational Living", *International Migration Review* Vol. 37, No. 3, pp. 666-699.

HANSON, G. (2010), "The *Governance of Migration Policy*", *Journal of Human Development and Capabilities*, Vol. 11, No. 2, pp. 185-207.

HATTON, T. (2007), "Should We Have a WTO for International Migration?" *Economic Policy*, Vol. 22, No. 50, pp. 339-383.

HATTON, T. and J. WILLIAMSON (2005), *Global Migration and the World Economy: Two Centuries of Policy and Performance*, MIT Press, Cambridge, MA.

HINOJOSA-OJEDA, R. (2010), *Raising the Floor for American Workers: The Economic Benefits of Comprehensive Immigration Reform*, Center for American Progress, American Immigration Council, Washington DC.

JACHIMOWICZ, M. (2006), "Argentina: A New Era of Migration and Migration Policy", *Migration Information Source*, Migration Policy Institute, Washington, DC, February.

JOHNSON, J. and M. REGETS (1998), "International Mobility of Scientists and Engineers to the US – Brain Drain or Brain Circulation?" *NSF Issue Brief* Vol. 98, No. 316, pp. 1-4.

KEELEY, B. (2009), *International Migration. The Human Face of Globalisation*, OECD, Paris.

KUZNETSOV, Y. and C. SABEL (2006), "International Migration of Talent, Diaspora Networks, and Development: Overview of Main Issues", in Y. KUZNETSOV, ed., *Diaspora Networks and the International Migration of Skills*, World Bank,Washington, DC., pp. 3-19.

MEYER, J.B. (2010), "La circulation des compétences, un enjeu pour le développement", *Annuaire suisse de politique de développement*, Vol. 27, No. 2, pp. 53-67.

MOSES, J. and B. LETNES (2004), "The Economic Costs to International Labor Restrictions: Revisiting the Empirical Discussion", *World Development*, Vol. 32, No. 10, pp. 1609-1626.

OECD (2004), *Trade and Migration: Building Bridges for Global Labour Mobility*, OECD, Paris.

OECD (2007a), *Policy Coherence for Development: Migration and Developing Countries*, OECD, Paris.

OECD (2007b), *Gaining from Migration: Towards a New Mobility System*, OECD, Paris.

OECD (2008), *International Migration Outlook 2008*, OECD, Paris.

OECD (2010), *International Migration Outlook 2010*, OECD, Paris.

OECD (2011a), *Perspectives on Global Development 2011: Shifting Wealth: An Opportunity for Social Cohesion?*, OECD, Paris.

OECD (2011b), *International Migration Outlook 2011*, OECD, Paris.

RICHTER, W. E. (2004), "Delaying Integration of Immigrant Labor for the Purpose of Taxation", *Journal of Urban Economics*, Vol. 55, pp.597-613.

SAß, B. (2010), "Immigration and Redistribution", in *Essays in Public Economics*, Universität Mannheim, Mannheim, pp. 7-37.

SADIQ, K. (2009), "Paper Citizens: How Illegal Immigrants Acquire Citizenship in Developing Countries", Oxford University Press, Oxford, 275 pp.

SHIMAN, D. (2009), "Human Rights Education in Costa Rica: More Expectation than Implementation", *Interamerican Journal of Education for Democracy*, Vol.2, No. 1, pp.30-51.

SINN, H. W. (2005), "Migration and Social Replacement Incomes: How to Protect Low Income Workers in the Industrialized Countries against the Forces of Globalization and Market Integration", *International Tax and Public Finance*, Vol. 12, pp.375-393.

TERRY, D. and S. WILSON (2005), *Beyond Small Change: Making Migrant Remittances Count*, Inter-American Development Bank, Washington, DC.

TODARO, M. (1969), "A Model of Labor Migration and Urban Unemployment in Less Developed Countries", *American Economic Review*, Vol. 59, No. 1, pp. 138-148.

TRACHTMAN, J. P. (2009), "The International Law of Economic Migration. Toward the Fourth Freedom", W.E. Upjohn Institute for Employment Research, Kalamazoo, MI, pp. 416.

UN-Habitat (2010), "State of the World's Cities 2010/2011: Bridging the Urban Divide", UN-Habitat, New York, NY.

VÁSQUEZ MOTA, J. (2005), "El Programa Iniciativa Ciudadana 3x1: un instrumento para respaldar la inversión social de los inmigrantes mexicanos", *Foreign Affairs en español* Vol. 5, No. 3, pp. 37-42.

WEIL, P. (2010), "All or Nothing? What the United States Can Learn from Europe as it Contemplates Circular Migration and Legalization for Undocumented Immigrants", *Immigration Paper Series*, German Marshall Fund of the United States.

ZWEIG, D. (2006), "Competing for Talent: China's Strategies to Reverse Brain Drain", *International Labour Review* Vol. 145, No. 1-2, pp. 65-89.

Chapter 6

Conclusion:
Towards effective partnerships

Abstract

The stalemate over the global governance of migration may be more apparent than real. It could be resolved by greater international co-operation: bilateral, regional and, in certain cases, global. Decentralisation is another element, as problems may be more effectively solved at the local level and if more actors are involved from all sectors of society. Migration policies should not be seen in isolation from others, such as those affecting agriculture, labour, trade and development. There are policy trade-offs to be made in the areas, for example, of trade and protectionism. Developing countries need to recognise that emigration brings social costs as well as financial benefits. There may be little incentive for governments to introduce necessary reforms. The example of several former origin countries shows the importance of implementing structural reforms rather than relying on migration. Even though it has a role to play, the challenge is to transform emigration into sustainable development at home.

Chapter 5 addressed the three policy challenges of international migration by formulating a governance framework based on a more flexible regulation of flows, a better integration of immigrants into society and a greater impact of labour mobility on development. It highlighted three specific issues:

- The mechanisms of compensation that should be associated with increased migration circularity;

- The good international practices adopted by developing countries to face the challenge of immigrant integration;

- The different instruments to minimise the lost-labour effect and maximise the remittance effect in migrant-sending countries.

This chapter lays the foundation of an efficient governance system of international migration based on effective partnerships and relying on four dimensions (Figure 6.1): international co-operation, decentralisation, inclusiveness and policy coherence.

Figure 6.1. **The four dimensions of the governance of migration**

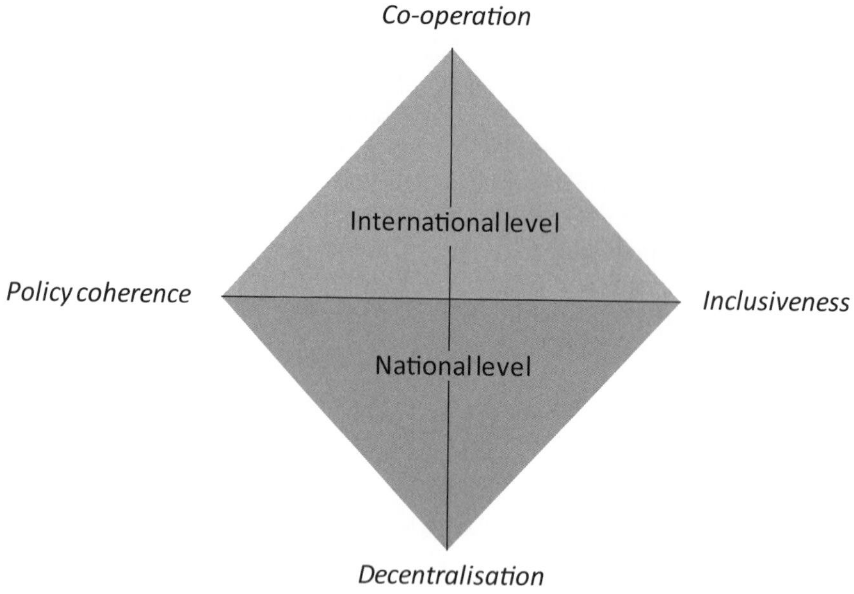

Fostering international co-operation

Chapter 2 showed that the current lack of international co-operation on migration issues is related to the asymmetry of benefits between high and low-income countries: workers from rich countries are generally less interested in moving to poorer countries. This problem of reciprocity has made reaching a consensus difficult within the international community, and it certainly explains why no multilateral body has been given the responsibility of regulating the movement of labour or even of co-ordinating migration policies.

However, the gridlock may be more illusory than real because:

- Countries of destination also benefit from immigration, which contributes both to economic growth and the financing of social protection systems;

- Strict border controls are costly, not only for migrant-sending countries, but also for the countries of destination;

- The countries of origin can also participate in the management of migration flows;

- Countries of immigration can leverage negotiations on migration to improve other key issues, such as environmental and social concerns.

There is, therefore, more room for co-operation than is generally admitted. Because of the interaction between the regulation of flows, the integration of immigrants and the development of the countries of origin, negotiations should go beyond the sole management of flows. Conversely, discussions on the migration-development nexus should not set aside the regulation of flows, as it is currently the case with the Global Forum on Migration and Development (see Box 2.2). Eventually country initiatives on international co-operation should apply a combination of bilateral, regional and global level agreements.

Bilateral level

The general objective of bilateral agreements is to increase efficiency in regulating flows while also maximising the developmental advantages of migration. In this way both sides have an incentive to engage in an agreement. It may take several forms, such as temporary worker programmes, joint efforts to encourage entrepreneurial activities in the home country, or readmission programmes.

The Spanish Temporary and Circular Labour Migration (TCLM) programme,[1] for instance, emphasises the development of the community of origin by supporting migrants with investment projects. Apart from their farming activities, circular workers benefit from specific training aimed at developing personal and collective investment projects. The accumulated savings by seasonal workers in Spain have helped foster the development of entrepreneurial activities such as the cultivation of fruits and cereals, investment in new techniques of farm management and the creation of social and cultural projects (IOM, 2010a).

Bilateral agreements can also help mitigate the negative effects of a brain drain. Countries of immigration can accelerate brain circulation by establishing grant programmes for students from developing countries conditional on their return, as done in the US Fulbright programme. In addition, training in areas of high demand in developing countries (e.g. agronomy, hydraulic engineering) should be encouraged, through financial aid and temporary work programmes (OECD, 2007a). Initiatives such as the TOKTEN programme (Transfer of Knowledge through Expatriate Nationals) should also be extended.[2]

Regional level

Despite the growing number of protocols on free movement (see Box 2.1), the actual movement of people remains hindered by administrative obstacles. While free movement of workers seems optimal on paper, in reality national concerns tend to trump regional ones, mostly for security-related reasons. For instance, ASEAN leaders adopted a Declaration on the Protection and Promotion of the Rights of Migrant Workers in 2007, but they were highly criticised during a forum on migration in Jakarta in 2011 for having done little to push it forward.[3]

Another problem is that immigrant integration and citizenship are being left out of regional discussions and are rarely a policy objective. Removing the barriers to movement is only half the equation of a successful regionally integrated labour force. As noted by Sadiq (2009), problems of citizenship are one of the primary reasons for the segregation of immigrants in society, the prevalence of informality and the high level of trafficking of illegal goods and people. The ambiguous notion of the path to citizenship has been a major determinant in many of the wars in West Africa, notably in Côte d'Ivoire.

Regions must continue to work to facilitate movement to maximise the new regional opportunities brought about by economic growth, demographic booms and globalisation. In this respect, regional co-operation should aim for functional labour liberalisation rather than a simple normative approach. This supposes the suppression of rigid formalities at the borders, making it easier and quicker to cross them legally. This would deter potential irregular immigrants from entering countries through informal channels.

Regions also need to work more closely together to help people get to the available jobs, enjoy the benefits of working, and minimise the exploitation of, and discrimination against, immigrants. Because the surest way to ensure integration is to get people jobs, the creation of regional job centres, which provide information directly to immigrants before emigration decisions are made, further reduces labour market frictions. Sending and receiving countries may also sign bilateral agreements to foster the international portability of pensions and social benefits (OECD, 2009), at least in the areas where such benefits actually exist.

Global level

Most countries are not willing to abandon part of their sovereignty and risk losing control over who crosses their borders. For this reason the creation of a World Migration Organisation (WMO) is unlikely. As seen above, a combination of local, regional and bilateral co-operation can mitigate the lack of global co-ordination. But certain elements of migration are better served at the global level and thus need to be handled as such.

One example is **environmental change**, which contributes to increasing both internal and international migration (see Chapter 1), and raises the importance of managing strategies of adaptation in the most affected countries. The issue of rising seawater for island states provides a good example of what a possible co-ordination failure on migration could lead to. The absence of an appropriate international response may make a large number of people stateless with no legal resource for entry elsewhere. In the absence of legal opportunities to emigrate, many of them are likely to turn into irregular migrants. Identifying patterns of migration and recognition of appropriate admission policies at the global level is thus crucial (Martin, 2010).

Expanding policies to include environmental refugees is also necessary (Myers, 2002). Some countries have enacted policies for environmental migrants, such as the US temporary protected status (TPS) programme. However the TPS is restricted to people already in the United States at the time of the natural disaster. It also only applies to situations that are temporary in nature. The TPS has therefore limited utility in addressing environmental migrants. In this respect, Sweden is one of the few countries including environmental migrants within its asylum system.

Humanitarian crises, forcing people out of their country, are another example where a global governance framework is necessary. The 2011 famine in Somalia, for instance, has led thousands of refugees to flee into Kenya, settling in camps, such as Dadaab, the largest refugee camp in the world (see Chapter 1). OECD countries should be able quickly to intervene, through increased logistical and financial aid, to help receiving countries face such crises.

Finally, several countries, such as Mexico, Morocco and Turkey, have become the focal point for thousands of **transit migrants** trying to reach richer and more stable economies (see Chapter 3). Because this situation is an indirect consequence of restrictive migration policies in richer countries, these should also share the burden of responsibility. One option is to provide assistance to transit countries not only to control migration, as is currently the case,[4] but also to help protect the basic rights of stranded and vulnerable migrants.

Strengthening decentralisation

Regulation and integration policies must be sufficiently decentralised to adapt to local needs and be embedded in the general local socio-economic development strategies (OECD, 2006). This is particularly true in many developing countries, where labour markets are relatively isolated and individual integration first plays out at the local level (see Box 5.1).

Under these circumstances, the onus largely falls on local and traditional leaders to help integrate and maximise social cohesion between old and new members of society. Local leaders are in the best position to understand their community's ability to shape social capital and reduce tension between immigrants and locals. This may include provisions that allow immigrants entering through informal channels to register locally with ease, a task which can be delegated to local leaders.

Furthermore, local authorities have better knowledge of local problems. In this sense, they may react faster and communicate strategies and solutions more quickly. Because authorities are closer to households, the potential for corruption may be lower, for altruistic reasons and also because managing smaller regions and groups is easier, and the reverse relationship – accountability – more binding. In addition, in many countries traditional leaders exercise more influence over households than does the central government. They may be more adapted to dealing with local customs, working habits, language, and business culture.

Finally, the decentralisation process implies that all administrative levels are better prepared to deal with all dimensions of migration, in particular through improved capacity building (IOM, 2010b). The fight against human trafficking, for instance, requires training of police and custom officers, but also of social workers and magistrates. In this respect, international co-operation can complement decentralisation and improve field capacity by enabling transfers of expertise. The IOM and the African Capacity-Building Centre, for instance, have been working closely with the Ghana Immigration Service in training border guards on migration management, trafficking and data collection. The training also focuses on working with local decision makers and on the particularities of each migration corridor.

Including more actors

Governance and government are not necessarily synonymous, and other institutions contribute to providing good governance (Dixit, 2009). Migration implies interaction between public and private institutions, where civil society plays a significant role. The role of civil society has typically revolved around the protection of migrant rights, but it should extend beyond in order to favour bottom-up and not only top-down governance (Newland, 2005).

Non-governmental organisations (NGOs)

Many NGOs help both regular and irregular immigrants face challenges in host countries. HTAs, in particular, represent an important support for fellow countrymen in receiving countries because:

- They may be more efficient in providing needed resources locally and directly to immigrants, such as clinical services and training;

- Messages need to come across quickly, particularly when tensions spiral out of control, and HTAs help communicate messages to large groups of immigrants;

- They also provide leadership for under-represented groups of society: for the many immigrants who do not speak or read the local language, they bring an aspect of representation and communication, for information-gathering or even for venting concerns about problems encountered;

- Cultural organisations become instruments of expression, helping share traditions and foster understanding within society.

Social organisations, private foundations or religious groups also help immigrants better understand arcane administrative procedures and integrate into host society. But because most of them act as a counterbalance to strict migration regulations they are generally excluded from the migration policy agenda. As a result they also act as an opposition force. Including them in discussions would help public authorities improve their knowledge of the experience of migrants, and would enable NGOs to make constructive proposals.

Trade unions

In the same way, but from a different perspective, trade unions should be included in any policy dialogue. Many foreign workers do not have access to union representation, either because they think they do not need it, because there is no culture of union organisation in their countries, or because unions themselves see immigrants as competitors for local workers (OECD, 2010). The risk is that some employers take advantage of the situation to break labour and wage regulations, for instance by not paying overtime.

The expertise of trade unions is therefore useful in improving the working conditions of immigrants and fighting against potential discrimination. In addition, trade unions can help promote dialogue with native workers to facilitate interaction with immigrants and reduce social tensions (OECD, 2007b). This supposes that foreign workers gain better access to union representation, but also that trade unions accept better to protect foreign workers.

The private sector

Private companies are directly concerned by migration policies, as border controls affect labour force supply, both quantitatively and qualitatively. For this reason they should be more involved in the decisions that concern work permits or temporary and return migration programmes. In this respect, employers' associations play a significant role in the shaping of immigration policies (OECD, 2010). As shown in Chapter 2, lobbying groups contribute to curbing migration restrictions: in the United States, a 10% increase in lobbying expenditures per native worker leads to a 3.1% to 5% increase in the number of visas (Facchini *et al.*, 2010).

The governance of migration should be extended to corporate governance, in particular with regard to the protection of the rights of migrant workers. Employers must proactively take part in the dialogue on migration reform and improving migrant rights. They also need to organise orientation programmes upon arrival, and improve international recruitment practices (BSR, 2009).

Academic sector

The gap between academic research and public decisions needs to be reduced. Most public authorities are not aware of the advances of migration-related research and therefore do not take them into account at the time of designing migration policies. Conversely, many researchers are not really concerned with the policy implications of their works. Seminars gathering policy makers and researchers make the dialogue easier. The public financing of policy-oriented research also helps bridge the gap and contributes to adopting more efficient migration policies.

Improving policy coherence

The governance of international migration should not only be based on migration policies, but also on other policies, such as agriculture, labour, trade and development (OECD, 2007a; UNDP, 2009). Policy coherence is indeed necessary to reach the objectives of regulation, integration and development, as analysed in this book. It concerns both the countries of destination and origin.

But one problem of immigration strategies is precisely the lack of coherence between policies. Even though the effects of trade and foreign aid on development are ambiguous (see Chapter 2), it may seem inconsistent to fight against immigration on the one hand while reducing development aid on the other. It does not make sense, either, to adopt policies linking migration and development while maintaining trade barriers. Trade protectionism, particularly in the agricultural and textile sectors, prevents developing countries from exploiting their comparative advantages and inserting themselves fairly into the global trade system (Cervantes-Godoy and Dewbre, 2010). It therefore contributes, at least indirectly, to the increase in South-North migration flows.

OECD countries need, therefore, to face the potential policy trade-offs by clearly defining their priorities. If the priority is to reduce labour inflow, then agricultural policies should aim at reducing subsidies so that developing countries may increase their competitiveness. Not only would such a policy generate employment in the rural areas of developing countries,[5] but it would also decrease the demand for low-skilled foreign labour in OECD countries.

But if border controls only represent a second-best option for other domestic priorities, such as saving jobs and preserving social cohesion, then policy makers should focus on these objectives through optimal policy intervention (Bhagwati, 1971). For instance, the best way to help low-skilled workers face international competition, induced either by international trade or labour mobility, is to invest in human capital instead of trying to protect the economy with trade or migration barriers. Likewise, immigration in itself does not represent a threat to social cohesion. It is rather the lack of specific housing, education and social measures to promote integration that makes it a problem.

Migrant-sending countries also need to take into account the interactions between migration policies and other economic and social areas. As seen in Chapter 4, the lost-labour effect induced by emigration is the result of missing or incomplete labour markets, especially in rural areas. Labour reforms should therefore encourage internal mobility, at both the geographical and sectoral levels. In the same way, policies aiming at increasing financial democracy help increase the benefits of remittances.

However, even though emigration may help foster development in the home country, it is not a foolproof strategy. The potential shortcomings of a strategy based on leveraging migration for development can be harmful and need to be taken into account. For instance, remittance-receiving economies may suffer from a "Dutch disease"-like problem, with increasing levels of dependency only satisfied through a permanent outflow of workers. When emigrants stop transferring money, the community of origin becomes vulnerable and the development model crumbles (see Box 4.3 for a recent illustration of this phenomenon).

In addition, migration-related policies usually focus on economic development, much to the detriment of the social dimension. Policies often emphasise the channelling of remittances towards productive investment and the return of high-skilled workers. But migration also comes with a social cost, such as the negative effects on those left behind, namely the young and the elderly, and can thus give rise to family disintegration (see Box 4.2).

Sending countries also risk falling into poverty traps. As long as emigration contributes to reducing demographic pressure and remittances feed the economy, governments have little incentive to undertake reforms. By helping partially solve unemployment problems, labour outflows undermine efforts to reform the labour market. As remittances provide informal social protection insurance, emigration countries also have less incentive to create a welfare state. Some countries may even want to encourage people to leave in order to reduce tension at home.

By contrast, successful countries have all carried out profound economic and social reforms. The achievements of such countries as Ireland, Spain or South Korea cannot be specifically attributed to the emigration process they experienced in the past, but rather to structural reforms. These countries, which used to export manpower, have become net receivers – or were until the recent crisis. This does not mean that emigration cannot help spur development, but the policy challenge here precisely consists in turning migration into sustainable development.

Notes

1. The TCLM has been implemented in Spain by the Fundación Agricultores Solidarios (FAS), in partnership with the Catalan fund for Co-operation and Development, the Agencia Española de Cooperación Internacional para el Desarrollo (AECID) and the International Organization for Migration (IOM). Bolivia, Colombia, Morocco, Romania and Senegal have been the main beneficiaries of the programme.

2. The TOKTEN programme (Transfer of Knowledge through Expatriate Nationals), launched by the UNDP in Turkey in 1977, allows qualified expatriates to return for weeks or months to their countries of origin to use their skills to benefit the community. Compared to more traditional programmes of co-operation, TOKTEN has the advantage of relying on professionals who already have knowledge of the language and culture of the country.

3. GMA News, 6 May 2011, "Civil society groups pushing for protection of ASEAN migrant workers", available at www.gmanews.tv/story/219837/pinoy-abroad/civil-society-groups-pushing-for-protection-of-asean-migrant-workers.

4. The risk behind the externalisation of policies is that transit countries may exploit their position as a "geopolitical opportunity" (Bredeloup and Pliez, 2011) to receive increased assistance, much to the detriment of migrant rights. This was, for instance, the case of Libya, which until the recent conflict received financial assistance from Italy and other European countries to prevent migrants from crossing the Mediterranean Sea. Human rights were far from a priority.

5. Anderson *et al.* (2011) argue that removing trade distortions would boost net farm incomes and raise real wages for unskilled workers in developing countries, hence reducing the number of poor people worldwide by 3%.

References

ANDERSON, K., J. COCKBURN and W. MARTIN (2011), "Would Freeing Up World Trade Reduce Poverty and Inequality? The Vexed Role of Agricultural Distortions", *World Bank Policy Research Working Paper* 5603, World Bank, Washington, DC.

BHAGWATI, J. (1971), "The Generalized Theory of Distortions and Welfare", in J. BHAGWATI *et al.* (eds.), *Trade, Balance of Payments and Growth*, North-Holland, Amsterdam.

BREDELOUP, S. and O. PLIEZ (2011), "The Libyan Migration Corridor", European University Institute.

BSR (Business Social Responsibility) (2009), *BSR Report 2008: Meeting the Challenge of a Reset World*, BSR.

CERVANTES-GODOY, D. and J. DEWBRE (2010), "Economic Importance of Agriculture for Poverty Reduction", *OECD Food, Agriculture and Fisheries Working Papers* 23, OECD, Paris.

DIXIT, A. (2009), "Governance Institutions and Economic Activity", *American Economic Review*, Vol. 99, No. 1, pp. 5-24.

FACCHINI, G., A.M. MAYDA and P. MISHRA (2010), "Do Interest Groups Affect US Immigration Policy?", *CReAM Discussion Paper* No. 04/09, Centre for Research and Analysis of Migration.

IOM (2010a), *Temporary and Circular Labour Migration: Experiences, Challenges and Opportunities*, IOM, Colombia, Bogota.

IOM (2010b), *World Migration Report 2010. The future of Migration: Building Capacities for Change*, IOM, Geneva.

MARTIN, S. (2010), "Climate Change, Migration and Governance", *Global Governance: A Review of Multilateralism and International Organizations*, Vol. 16, No. 3, pp. 397-413.

MYERS, N. (2002), "Environmental Refugees: A Growing Phenomenon of the 21st Century", *Philosophical Transactions of the Royal Society B: Biological Sciences*, Vol. 357, No. 1420, pp. 609-613.

NEWLAND, K. (2005), "The Governance of International Migration: Mechanisms, Processes and Institutions", *Working paper, Policy Analysis and Research programme*, Global Commission on International Migration.

OECD (2006), *From Immigration to Integration: Local Solutions to a Global Challenge*, Local Economic and Employment Development (LEED), OECD, Paris.

OECD (2007a), *Policy Coherence for Development: Migration and Developing Countries*, OECD, Paris.

OECD (2007b), *Gaining from Migration: Towards a New Mobility System*, OECD, Paris.

OECD (2009), *Latin American Economic Outlook 2010*, OECD, Paris.

OECD (2010), *International Migration Outlook 2010*, OECD, Paris.

SADIQ, K. (2009), "Paper Citizens: How Illegal Immigrants Acquire Citizenship in Developing Countries", Oxford University Press, Oxford.

UNDP (2009), *Human Development Report 2009. Overcoming Barriers: Human Mobility and Development*, UNDP, Palgrave Macmillan, New York, NY.